TWELVE
LIGHT YEARS

Buchan Ness Lighthouse at lime-washing time

TWELVE
LIGHT YEARS

Margaret Aitken

Illustrated by
Ian MacInnes

ALBYN PRESS

© Margaret Aitken 1988

Made and printed in
Great Britain
and published by
ALBYN PRESS
(Charles Skilton
Publishing Group)
Whittingehame House
Haddington, East Lothian

ISBN 0284 98776 X

Dedicated with love to Jimmy
because of everything,
and written especially for Richard, Katherine and Ray

Acknowledgements

I wish to thank the following:-

J. M. Dent & Sons Ltd for permission to quote from *Fishing Boats and Fisher Folk on the East Coast of Scotland* by Peter Anson, published 1930.

Robson Books Ltd, Publishers, for permission to quote from *More Morley* by Robert Morley.

The Editor of *The Countryman* for permission to reprint material which appeared in that magazine in articles by me, and *The Scots Magazine* for permission to draw on my articles published by that magazine.

The kind people of Boddam who spoke to me about their village.

David Toulmin, the author, for his help, support, encouragement and constructive criticism.

My friend, Michael Ross, for listening patiently to my doubts and urging me to go on writing.

My family — Jimmy, Richard and Katherine — for their help, support, encouragement and constructive criticism, and a special thank you to Katherine who took over the housekeeping to let me type it all out.

Prologue

"FAIR Rachel dwelt in her high tower" while the waves dashed themselves against its base, and the winds rocked the slender length of it. Her only contact with humanity was by a telephone link with her guardians far away on the distant shore.

But Rachel, like so many of her kind, was temperamental, and her guardians became dissatisfied with her, hauled her from her refuge, and gave it to a young, efficient male.

Should anything cause him discomfiture he cries out to the distant guardians for help, and each day just after the setting of the sun they lift their telephone and listen while he reports his condition to them in the code in which he is bound to express himself: "Station A — Normal", if all is well, and they reply with a high pitched whistle which indicates to him that the time for communicating is over — they do not wish to hear another word.

Who are these unusual people, you may well ask? They sound like characters out of science fiction. But no — you're not embarking on a science fiction story. The guardians of the hermit are lightkeepers at Kinnaird Head Lighthouse, Fraserburgh, Aberdeenshire, Scotland, and the hermit is one of the robots who are gradually taking over the lighthouses all round the coasts of our country. This particular robot is in the tower of Rattray Head Lighthouse which stands on a lonesome rock about half a mile off the north-east coast of Aberdeenshire.

At the time of "Rachel", as the keepers called the female voice that reported to them, the gadget alerted them to any misdemeanour in the light emitted by "three banks of locomotive headlights on a rotating platform"; or in the fog sensor that, by its electronic beam sent out every five minutes, decided if visibility was such that the foghorn outside the tower needed to switch itself on and sound its warning note to mariners. The male-voiced piece of equipment no doubt does the same but more efficiently than "Rachel" which it replaced.

It's because of the robots' take-over that I am writing this story. It will be as true an account as I can make it of a way of life that is surely passing away — life at a lighthouse as seen by a lightkeeper's wife.

If things go on as they are doing, future lighthouses will have no keepers, never mind wives, living beside them. Indeed, should I even think *future* lighthouses?

In our local newspaper the other day there appeared a heading, "Lighthouses not necessary, say ship operators". At present the case put forward by the Northern Lighthouse Board's commissioners for installing four automatic lights on the Outer Hebrides' Atlantic coast, and the opposing argument of the General Council of British Shipping, are before the relevant government minister.

The view of the General Manager of the Northern Lighthouse Board is, that this, the regular route of oil tankers plying between Sullom Voe oil terminal in Shetland and southern ports, and the traditional working area of a great number of fishing boats, requires lighthouses to prevent disasters which might end with pollution of the Outer Hebrides.

Ship operators claim that modern tankers have "such reliable electronic navigation equipment" that lights on the coast are no longer needed.

The Government minister has ordered a traffic survey of the area. The Northern Lighthouse Board say they have based their plans on a computer study carried out in 1978.

It would seem that even the robot keepers are now threatened.

10

I feel the time has come for me to try to put on record how I found life in the lighthouse service from 1954 to 1966, in the days before the switches and black boxes, or, as I think of it, before lighthouses were de-humanised and certainly before the need for their existence was ever in doubt.

Now I'll begin at the beginning of the story proper.

Chapter One

THERE was to be a wedding in Kirkwall, Orkney and I, in a long dress of peach silk with autumn flowers in my hair, was to be bridesmaid.

One day, when looking at the latest presents to arrive at the brides home, I noticed a tea-set with a card saying "From James and John Aitken".

"Who are they?" I asked.

"They come from Deerness," explained the bride. "One has a garage, and the other has something to do with the lighthouse on Copinsay." She went on to say that the latter was going "to do a monologue" at the wedding.

I remarked, "Oh dear," feelingly, for I usually found such amateur performances embarrassing to witness.

The night of the wedding arrived. It was a real Orkney wedding — at least as real as one in an urban setting could be compared to the traditional country kind.

The church ceremony took place in the early evening to be followed by eating, dancing, merry-making, and the passing round of the "bride's cog" until the dawn broke. The "bride's cog" was a wooden tub with handles filled with a heated, spicy mixture of alcoholic beverages passed round the company from hand to hand, each person taking a sip from it, before handing it on.

At intervals between dances, guests sang and played musical instruments, and at last the one "to do the monologue" was announced, and he, to my surprise, performed really well. I also noted that he was tall, slim and altogether a very attractive young man.

I took the first opportunity as I was whisked past him in a dance, to breathe "Congratulations". And it worked — for with the announcement of the next dance he arrived to partner me. A romance had begun.

For three years, Jimmy and I got to know each other. Every other evening he sped the ten miles from his parish of Deerness to my home in Kirkwall on his International Norton motor-bike.

We talked of how to obtain a house when neither party had any money. Jimmy had worked since the age of fourteen on his father's small farm. There was no house available there, and anyhow no possibility of forty acres providing for two households. Besides, I couldn't milk a cow, and had been terrified of hens ever since a farmer's wife invited me as a child of about three to go with her and feed the hens. She opened the door of a black-tarred hen-house and out flew a screeching rooster, his claws scraping my head. I was terrified, and have never since been able to stand birds close to me, and definitely not indoors.

Then there was Jimmy's second job, that of Occasional Lightkeeper on the island of Copinsay which lay about three miles across the sea from his home. He had been employed in this capacity for two years, going to the island

14

to take the place of any lightkeeper off duty for any reason. Now we wondered if his joining the Northern Lighthouse Service as a professional keeper was our best plan. Certainly it would mean we'd be provided with a house.

One dark, winter's night we debated the matter right up to the post-box a short distance from my parents' home. Jimmy, letter for application form in hand, said, "Will I?" I said, "Yes." He posted the letter, and set going the process that led to our twelve years in the Northern Lighthouse Service.

Not long after this, Jimmy was summoned to the office of the Northern Lighthouse Board in George Street, Edinburgh, where he had to take a general knowledge test, undergo a medical examination, and be interviewed by the Secretary to the Board.

Jimmy's mother had decided for some reason that he'd be sent to remote Cape Wrath, and packed his case accordingly with enough clothes, food and medical supplies for a long stay in isolation.

However, on being accepted into the Northern Lighthouse Service, he was sent forthwith to Kinnaird Head Lighthouse on the edge of the shop-filled streets of Fraserburgh, to receive training as a Supernumerary Keeper.

Vaccination against smallpox put his one arm out of action so that when he was ordered to move to the lighthouse of Dubh Artach, a tower perched on a rock on the west coast of Scotland, Mr Allan Firth, the Principal Lightkeeper at Kinnaird Head, had to say he was unfit for the derrick landing, which involved clinging to a rope by hands and feet while the lightkeepers on the rock hoisted him ashore from the ship by means of a crane on the landing place. So he was kept at Kinnaird Head a little longer.

He asked me to come south from Orkney before he was

moved on. I suggested he book me into a hotel near the lighthouse, but the Principal Keeper, Mr Firth, and his wife would not hear of this arrangement, and invited me to stay with them. Mr Allan Firth was a tall, heavily built man. His wife was a small, dainty, silver-haired lady, and both were the epitome of the kindness I was to find abounded in the Lighthouse Service.

The lighthouse at Kinnaird Head is unusual in that its tower protrudes from a sixteenth century tower-keep — all that remains of a castle built there by Sir Alexander Fraser, the founder of the town of Fraserburgh. Sir Alexander's dungeons and servants' quarters were now used as a coal cellar, and the great hall of the castle, with minstrels' gallery still intact, served as a workshop and paraffin store.

In 1787, the first of the Northern Lighthouse Board's lighthouses was opened, when the most powerful light of its time was displayed from a lantern placed above the fourth floor of the original castle on Kinnaird Head.

The Supernumerary's room was in the castle, and said by some to have been the boudoir of Lady Saltoun. It was a large, grey room with a huge, black range in the fireplace and a small bed bought or made to fit into an alcove. Jimmy, (five feet ten inches tall) had to lie diagonally to fit into it, but he said his plight was not nearly as bad as that of his predecessor who had measured considerably over six feet.

I have never experienced cold as severe as it was that December weekend in Fraserburgh. The winds that whipped through the streets felt as though they were sweeping off ice, and cut through one like a knife.

We huddled beside the big. black, glowing range on which Jimmy did his cooking. A short, narrow passage led off the room to a little, circular turret in which he did his washing up.

As we sat there I remarked uneasily on the strange noises that pervaded the place. Jimmy said, "Och, that's the machine you're hearing. Let's go and take a look at it."

We left the room, climbed a short flight of stone steps, and arrived in the lightroom where the great, glittering, glass lens rumbled round the hissing paraffin lamp, and when the lightkeeper on watch wound up the clockwork machine that powered the lens, a heavy, metal weight rattled up the endless chain that dangled in the well of the stairs, and, with a loud clang, reached its fully wound position. My "strange sounds" were no longer a mystery.

Jimmy and I went out on the balcony that encircles the tower. A giant cartwheel of golden light revolved in the night sky above us. I trembled with awe as I had done when as a child in Orkney I had dared to look up at the shivering *aurora borealis*. Now this magnificent, man-made northern light produced the same effect.

Back in the supernumerary's room we became officially engaged.

We showed the Firths my beautiful, antique engagement ring, three diamonds set in a broad, gold band. The next day, Mrs Firth concocted for lunch a delicious, cold sweet which she called "Engagement Dessert".

We talked of the Lighthouse Service. There were three kinds of station — those, like Kinnaird Head on the Scottish mainland, where lightkeepers' wives could stay with their husbands; island stations where again they stayed together; and rock stations where the men did only two months of duty "on the rock", followed by a month ashore in a town on the nearest mainland, where houses were provided for their families.

I expressed the hope that we'd be posted where we'd be together. The Firths agreed that this was best. They had not especially liked the times they'd been apart, but Mr Firth, in his cheerful, philosophical way, said — "If it's a

17

rock, remember there's always the homecoming."

With a heavy heart I left Jimmy, and returned to our native Orkney.

A week or two after my visit, Jimmy was sent about nine miles south along the coast to Rattray Head Lighthouse.

Rattray is a pillar rock lighthouse. In 1893 there was constructed on the Ron Rock a great, circular lower section of stout, granite blocks. This section was fifty-five feet in diameter and forty-six feet high. The area on top of this section is known as "the quarter deck", and from it rises the more slender part of the building — a tower with a base diameter of twenty-one feet and a height of sixty-nine feet. This lighthouse was commissioned and opened in 1895.

In Jimmy's time the bottom section housed the engines that drove the foghorn which was mounted on "the quarter deck".

The more slender tower, which concluded 120 feet above the rock with lightroom, lantern and dome, contained storage space for coal, water and foodstuffs, the kitchen-cum-living room and sleeping accommodation. We were once asked if the beds were curved to fit into the walls of the tower, but Jimmy explained that the two bedrooms had a straight, central, partitioning wall on each side of which were three bunk beds.

No doubt there were times when six beds were needed, as when the annual overhaul of the engines and the inspection of the station was done by two engineers and a superintendent sent from the headquarters of the Northern Lighthouse Service in Edinburgh.

However, most of the time only three bunks were in use, for the light was manned by a Principal Keeper, two Assistants and a Supernumerary Keeper. Each of the three permanent staff did a four-week spell of duty on the rock, and then went ashore to his home behind the sand dunes for a fortnight. Jimmy was never off the rock during his stay of two months, and assured me he was perhaps the most comfortably situated person in the country, for the rest of us were enduring a severe winter of snow-storms and gale force winds.

The relief of the rock was made by the "boatman" driving a tractor and trailer over the sea-bed when, at new moon and full moon, the tides ebbed far out from the Aberdeenshire shore.

The returning keeper climbed a vertical iron ladder, three quarters of the height of the base, to enter the light-house by two doors in the twelve feet thick granite wall. Between the doors was the lavatory — a bucket on a rope long enough to reach the sea for "flushing". The foodstuffs, coal, water and mails were winched up to "the quarter deck" by a crane.

On Rattray three hour watches were kept by each man in turn — for fog throughout the daylight hours, and to attend to the light as well through the night. The usual lightkeeping duties were carried out — cleaning and main-taining the building itself and the care and operation of the equipment it contained. On top of this daily work the Supernumerary Keeper and Assistant took week about doing the cooking and house-cleaning.

One of the assistants had been a cook on a liner before joining the Lighthouse Service. He came to the rock armed with glossy cook books, but since their recipes demanded rather more exotic ingredients than there was to hand they did not effect much change in the menus. The "clootie" dumpling still went on to boil at the change of the watch at 3 am, and the man taking over at 6 am was charged to see it kept on boiling. I sent them the excellent little *Dundee Cookery Book*, and soon scones and cakes were being success-fully produced.

Up to a short time prior to that about which I am writing,

19

the large roasts had had to be sealed with melted fat on the cut end, to preserve them. Then a paraffin fuelled refrigerator was installed.

The Lighthouse Service provided regular reading material such as *The Illustrated London News, Chambers's Journal, The Argosy* and *Blackwood's Magazine.* These were passed on from station to station. There was also a library box provided.

Besides reading avidly, the men occupied their leisure hours with various hobbies. Some of them did woodwork in a workshop section in the base. Jimmy enjoyed working at marquetry, and made quite a few pictures. One I particularly liked, and still have hanging up, was of a yacht sailing on quiet grey waters. I was not greatly taken with a stag in the mountains — too reminiscent of Landseer. The First Assistant, George Robertson, made himself a button key accordion, and thereafter gave musical entertainment.

However, music was not the only sound to pervade Rattray. Wild winds howled, rough seas roared and the whole tower shuddered under their impact many a time, but every now and again there came another, more sinister sound. It was a strange moan that made itself heard throughout the building. The first time Jimmy heard it he was alone in the lightroom. He thought it must be the crying of seals on the rocks and went out on the balcony to look. It was a clear, still, moonlit night, but not a seal was to be seen. The second time the sound occurred he was with the Principal Lightkeeper, Mr Robert Oliver. "What is that?" Jimmy asked. "We don't know," said the Principal, and he went on to tell how they had carefully checked and oiled every bit of machinery in case this was the source.

Every other evening I rang the St Fergus number that put me through to the pillar rock lighthouse.

Then one night came the news I was eagerly awaiting.

20

Jimmy had received a letter appointing him to be an Assistant Lightkeeper, and ordering his transfer from Rattray Head to Stroma Lighthouse.

I knew that Stroma was an island somewhere in the Pentland Firth. In recent years several of the home island stations had been converted to operate as rock stations, wives and children being accommodated in houses provided in towns. So, my first anxious question was, "Will we be together?" Happily the answer was "Yes." Stroma still had a normal island station. Jimmy and I would be together there.

Chapter Two

IT WAS January 1955 when Jimmy received his posting to Stroma. He was to come home on leave, and then join the lighthouse ship *Pole Star* at the town of Stromness in Orkney.

The ships belonging to the Northern Lighthouse Board have such appropriate and lovely names. *Pole Star* after the yellow, supergiant star of the northern hemisphere; *Hesperus* after the beautiful star of the evening; *May* after the Isle of May in the Firth of Forth, the site of a lighthouse as early as 1635; and *Pharos* — the flag-ship bearing the name of the famous lighthouse at Alexandria, remembered as one of the seven wonders of the ancient world.

The lightkeepers' prayer was said to begin "Our fathers which art in Edinburgh," for it was from the office in George Street that all commands, rules, replies to requests and queries and provision for many needs came. All correspondence with those august beings was carefully signed — "I am Sir, Your obedient servant." Happily for us, "our fathers in Edinburgh" not only provided a house, but enough furniture, bedding, cooking equipment etc. to make life possible in it. We bought only two fireside chairs, some cake tins, a bread bin, an invaluable utensil known as a self-basting roasting tin and a roll of "congoleum", the least expensive form of floor-covering we could obtain.

Everything was packed and ready when a snow-storm blasted down on Orkney. Jimmy was at his parents' farm, "Delday", Deerness, ten miles away from me in Kirkwall and twenty-four miles from Stromness and the ship. I wept for I felt sure I would not see him before he went away to Stroma. However, to my great delight, he limped into town some time in the afternoon, one of his legs stiff and sore from trudging miles through deep snow in blizzard conditions. All roads were completely blocked.

Jimmy phoned the master of the *Pole Star* who said the ship would sail round to Scapa pier and collect him and his effects. The road from Scapa pier to Kirkwall was always kept cleared as it was the route to the only hospital. And so, Jimmy and all our worldly goods — a few tea boxes and a roll of "congoleum" on the back of a lorry — departed for Scapa pier.

The next day the fates were again on our side. The school where I taught was closed because of the weather conditions, and Jimmy phoned to say the ship was to remain in Stromness for the day. Stormy conditions prevailed round Stroma and it was not possible to make a landing there. As they say "Love laughs at locksmiths". I discovered that the snow plough had been through the Kirkwall to Stromness road and traffic was once again passing between the two towns, so, without a thought for icy roads or possible imminent snowfalls that might have prevented my return for days, I caught the next bus to Stromness.

The ice-rutted roads were festooned with power lines blown down by the storm. Stromness was trimming its lamps. Never mind, to us the wintry streets were beautiful. I don't remember even feeling cold. It was one of those blissful interludes that occur so rarely in life — those completely unexpected treats that must be seized and relished out of a life-time. We had afternoon tea in front of a blazing fire — just the two of us — in a comfortable little sitting room in the Stromness Hotel.

This was goodbye for no snow blocked my return to Kirkwall, and the next day the *Pole Star* did sail for Stroma. The weeks passed slowly. I dated my class register right up to the summer holidays and counted how many weeks we still had to be apart as I marked up one each Friday. My thoughts frequently turned to lighthouses.

With his spells on Copinsay, and a life-time of meeting lightkeepers and their families as they passed through his home parish of Deerness on their way to and from the island, Jimmy had a good idea of what he was letting himself in for. My knowledge of lighthouses and of island life was scant.

Glimpses of those pure white towers, aloof and alone on remote places, always put me in mind of story book castles. I had visited only one. That was Noup Head Lighthouse on the Orkney north isle of Westray, and I was four at the time.

My parents and I walked miles from the hotel in the village of Pierowall to Noup Head. The outward journey and the outside of the lighthouse, perhaps surprisingly, left no lasting impression, but the inside remained in my mind as a place of dazzling white walls, hung about with gleaming and sparkling objects, and containing a hard,

24

bare, stone stair that spiralled upwards higher and even higher. I plodded on, step after step, round and round, till my head began to spin and I thought I was going to be sick. The lightkeeper picked me up and bore me dizzily to the top. I was torn between gratitude for his assistance and unease at being held so close to a stranger.

However, the miles back to our base had me beat. Soon my short legs were aching with weariness. Almost weeping with fatigue, I sat down by the side of the road, and, despite my parents' hearty, jollying remarks, refused to proceed. By and by, a horse and cart trundled towards us. My father signalled it to stop, and asked the driver if he'd give me a lift. Assent given, I was heaved into the midst of a cart-load of carrot-haired children.

We lurched to the parting of our ways when I once more took up my marching position between my parents.

As we approached the village in the gathering dusk, a hump-backed figure strode past us. I wanted to know what kind of person that was. "It's a hiker," whispered my father, and I, not knowing what he meant, felt the hairs prick at the back of my neck.

Gratefully, I entered the safe, warm, lamp-lit hotel. But new experiences weren't over yet. To reach our room we had to pass through the dining room. At the white-clothed table sat a man and woman, and in front of them stood a huge hunk of pinkish beef streaked with blood. I couldn't believe my eyes. Rare meat was outwith my ken. In the privacy of our room my father enquired, "Did you see the beef? Those people are English and they like their meat with the blood still running through it."

It had been a strange day!

It was years later that I saw my second lighthouse and, as with the first, its associations were, for me, rather unusual.

As a family we were holidaying at a relative's house in the east mainland Orkney parish of Tankerness. One day we cycled to the neighbouring parish of Deerness. From there we looked over the sea to the island of Copinsay, a green hill-side sloping gently up out of the water. Perched on the middle of the hill-top was the snow-white lighthouse tower and its accompanying buildings, like an icing sugar model for a Christmas cake. Down near the shore was a brown, stonework building which was pointed out as having been the home of an enormous family of cousins. There were fourteen of them, and, a fact which greatly interested me, they had had a teacher all to themselves.

One day, some time before our viewing of Copinsay, two of those cousins and their mother arrived from the island to visit us in Kirkwall. To me they were "big girls". I was told to take them into the garden.

Now our garden was not at all of the adventure playground variety. Neat concrete paths transversed it, and children were expected to keep to them or play sedately on the lawn-cum-drying green.

Well, to begin with, my cousins and I walked along the paths. All was in order until we came to a barrel with a tap and a wooden trough — both the receptacles of carefully preserved rain water. Beside them stood a collection of jugs, kettles and tea-pots for applying the water to the garden. To my dismay my guests set to with a will to fill, spill and pour water. I can't remember if I joined in or not, but it did appear to be a grand occupation. Anyhow, after they'd gone, retribution fell. I should not have allowed it to happen, I was informed. "They're likely used to playing in water on Copinsay," was the excuse for the visitors. Copinsay sounded a desirable place.

Yes, from the little I knew I liked the sound of lighthouses and islands.

It is amazing how little friends know of each other. I was surprised at the number of mine who thought I had taken leave of my senses. "Whatever will you do on Stroma?" "I

26

give you six weeks of it." "There'll be nothing to do."
"There'll be nowhere to go." "You'll be lonely." "What
on earth will happen if you take appendicitis?" And so on
and so on.

At long last the summer and end of the school session
came.

We were married in Kirkwall on the 8 July 1955. A day
of fog I noted with dismay on getting up, but by noon as I,
all a-tremble, drove to the church with my father, the sky
had cleared and it was a beautiful sunny day. I continued
to shake like a leaf till the moment I saw Jimmy as he stood
waiting by the communion table. Then a joyous calm filled
me. When I told him of this, he teased, "Did you think I
mightn't turn up?"

Our reception was a very unremarkable affair — lunch
in the Lynnfield Hotel on the outskirts of Kirkwall with
relatives mainly. We then spent a few quiet days in the
parish of Birsay on the west side of the Orkney mainland so
that we were able to return easily and quickly to my
parents' home, and pack up our wedding gifts to take to
Stroma. I said to Jimmy's mother that I could hardly wait
to get there. She replied, "No wonder with all the bonnie
new things you have to work with." But there was more to
it than that, there was a feeling of starting on an adventure,
of life taking an exciting turning.

We took the aeroplane to Wick. By and by Jimmy said to
me — "There's Stroma." I looked down, and there below
us lay the island about two and a half miles long by a mile
or so wide. It basked in the blue sea like the gently raised
back of some somnolent sea creature. A long, low neck
stretched south and west in the direction of the Queen
Mother's Castle of Mey. To the north a short, flat tail
slipped into the Pentland Firth, and on this tail the trim
lighthouse tower and its accompanying buildings were set
like some glistening, pure white encrustation.

27

The BEA Pionair set us down at the aerodrome at Wick, and we spent the night in that town. In the morning we hired a taxi to take us the eighteen or so miles to a place called Huna — about a mile west of John o' Groats. On our arrival there I was dismayed to find that the scene of the previous day had undergone a drastic change. Where, from the air, we had looked down on a smooth, blue ribbon of water separating the island from the north coast of Scotland there was now a grey-green ruff of tossing sea. The wind tore white spray from the surface like lengths of coarse thread. The taxi driver, an ex-islander, added nothing to my peace of mind when he enquired, "Will ye no' be feard ower there when the whowl place shaks i' the winter time?"

A smithy, the smith's house and the remains of an old lifeboat shed were the only buildings at the landing place. Sheltering from the gusting wind beside the lifeboat shed we watched a dark shape buffet its way to shore. At last it materialised beside the disued lifeboat slipway as a small, open motor-boat. Jimmy tells me it measured twenty feet over the top.

Bearded, oilskin clad figures jumped ashore, and strode up the slip-way. A great many of the Stroma men had worn beards ever since Jimmy had come to the island. Beards were not in fashion in 1955 — at least, not in our part of the world. Jimmy had quite a shock when, attending his first funeral on the island, the company turned up clean shaven, and all at once unrecognisable.

Our luggage was stowed away in the hold of the boat, and I was tucked away beside it. A tarpaulin was laid over all. This I discovered was to be my position on all crossings which were described euphemistically as "a bit splashy," until I equipped myself with yellow oilskin and sou'wester, and, looking like an advertisement for John West's salmon,

28

pointed out that I was as suitably dressed to stay on deck as everybody else.

However, on that first crossing we bucked and heaved and rolled and tumbled our way across the two miles or so of the Sound. It was dark in the hold, which was pervaded with a mixture of smells — oil, tar, ropes, fish among them. Spray splattered on the tarpaulin like showers of hailstones. It seemed a long time, and I was sick, before the tarpaulin was lifted, and we were tied up to a pier.

Awaiting us was a battered lorry in the cab of which I was given a seat beside the one-legged lorry driver known as "Crooked John". We jolted and bumped our way up a stony road past stone houses spaced out at the road side, a church with manse attached, and a telephone kiosk.

We stopped beside a cream and green wooden building — the shop which belonged to the Scottish Wholesale Co-operative Society, and here supplies were unloaded. Then on again we "joldered". Stone houses with two or three rooms, many in ruins, stood by the roadside and over the fields, but a short, stocky fraction of the lighthouse tower was all we saw of our destination until we were right above it on the island's final most northerly bump. Downhill we sped through the main gate and, in a maelstrom of gravel, drew up in the forecourt of a block of three flat-roofed, white houses beside the tall tower of the lighthouse.

We hurried into our house — the central one in the block. It had four main rooms. There were two rooms in the front of the house and two at the back plus a tiny scullery. At the end of the front central passageway that ran from the front and only outside door, and between the two back rooms, was a big, walk-in cupboard. The back room with scullery off was our kitchen-cum-living room. The other was our bedroom. The one front room was our sitting room and the other was the "Occasional's Room".

The lavatory — a normal flush one — was housed in one of three cells at the extreme end of another block of buildings which consisted of the paint and joinery "shop", three stores where the often-needed packing boxes and such were kept and the three coal cellars.

Jimmy had been busy painting in the house. There was not much choice of paint among that provided for the station. We had decided by post, to have the living room cream, including the margins of floor surrounding the "congoleum" square — a completely impractical notion of mine as I soon found out. For the scullery, where the sink was installed, we had chosen cream and grey. Our bedroom and the sitting room were grey, and the "Occasional's Room" was cream.

The "Occasional's Room" was so called because this was where a keeper slept who was employed "occasionally" to replace one of the permanent staff in case of illness or holiday.

The furniture was old-fashioned and to my mind all the better for being so. There was a pine sideboard, oak tables and wardrobes and iron bedsteads with brass knobs — all of which nowadays would be valued highly and much sought after. Not that value entered my mind at the time. I just liked the look of the furniture and its plain good honest quality.

The rooms which were to be used as bedrooms were pre-determined by the presence of bells. When a keeper had to go on watch the man in the tower or engine room rang a bell which sounded in the bedroom. There was an un-written law that the bed had to be positioned so that the keeper had to get out to press the bell pushes and to answer his colleague in tower and engine room.

The bell never annoyed or startled me. Indeed it was rather nice to half-waken at midnight or 3 am or 6 am and know one didn't have to get up. Not so nice for the one who had to get up and go outside, no matter what the weather, to take over the watch for the next three hours.

On our arrival the Principal Lightkeeper had greeted us with an invitation to come and have tea with his family. Therefore, after a quick inspection of our house we went next door to meet our neighbours.

The "Principal", Mr John Lamont, was a slim, quiet spoken, mild mannered man. His wife was a short, plumpish lady with dark, flashing eyes. The Lamonts had a daughter, Mary, of about nine or ten years old, and a charming Shetland collie called Monty.

Mary turned out to be a really slick counter as a result of constant games of "Rummy" with Donald, the First Assistant.

It was she who mystified me by talk of "the shoe-box wifie". This turned out to be the name given to gentle-women who, at the instigation of an official of Missions to Seamen, sent a shoe-box full of gifts to lightkeepers and their families at Christmas. I felt quite indignant, thought the whole thing smacked of charity, and informed the official concerned that we did not wish to be "adopted" by a "shoe-box wifie". However, being of a very forceful, persistent turn of mind he went on his own way, and we duly received our shoe-box from a lady in Haslemere, Surrey. However, I didn't learn all this until later.

The First Assistant Keeper, Donald Macaulay, came to join us. He was a tall, handsome, red-haired man from the Western Isles with the attractive lilt of that region in his voice.

There was talk of supply days. Twice a week a boat crossed to Huna, and collected stock there from the shop. Those supplies had been transported from the town of Wick. Three times a week a boat crossed to collect mails from the Huna Post Office — weather permitting.

Those last two words were to become so important, as did "depending on the tide".

In the far-off days when Norse Earls ruled Orkney and Caithness, Stroma was known as Straumsey — the island in the current. Dependent as they were on sails and oars, the Norsemen knew full well that the seas around Stroma were forces to be reckoned with.

The flood tide runs east from Atlantic Ocean to North Sea for six hours. When at their strongest, in March and August, the spring tides can reach a velocity of eleven or twelve knots. At the west of Stroma the flood tide divides, one convulsion sweeping past the north end of the island, and one through the Inner Sound. Should there be an easterly swell as the flood forces its way into the Inner Sound, great walls of water built up by the swell break against the rushing tide from the West and East Bores. On the east side of Stroma an eddy is formed, in which flow currents, known at the north end as "The Ram", "Nor' Berth" and "The Peerie Nor' Berth", and at the south end as "The Farra Coo" and "The Wester Berth".

The ebb tide flows west and splits on the east side of the island. Again a current filled eddy is formed, this time on the west side of the island, and the currents are called "The Lang Berth" and "The Sou' Berth". It is then too that "the eyes" of the tide appear, "The Merry Men of Mey", "Sgeir Gal" off Beacon Point and "Well of Scartoun" on south side, "Sgeir Bhan" and "The Swelkie" to the north.

There is an old Norse legend about how the Swelkie originated. At the time of the birth of Christ there was a King of Denmark, then known as Gotland, called Frode. Under the influence of the Roman Emperor Augustus peace prevailed, but in the north this time of law and order was attributed to King Frode and the Danes, and Norsemen spoke of the "Peace of Frode".

King Frode heard of two maidservants, belonging to a king called Fjolner, who were renowned for their large size and enormous strength.

At that time two gigantic millstones were found in Denmark, so huge and heavy that no-one was able to turn them. They were situated in a mill called Grotte, and they had the magical property of being able to grind whatever the miller asked of them.

Frode purchased the two giant girls, Fenja and Menja, and took them to the mill of Grotte. There he instructed them to grind gold and peace and happiness for him. He didn't show much care for their happiness, making them toil at the mill with hardly any rest or sleep.

They took their revenge for this harsh treatment. While they sang their "Grotte-song" they ground out an army to fight Frode. That night Mysing the sea-king came to lead the army, slew Frode, and made off with much plunder including the Grotte, Fenja and Menja.

However, Mysing too was greedy. He ordered them to grind salt as his ship carried them away. In the middle of the night Fenja and Menja enquired if he now had enough salt. He ordered them to continue grinding, but they hadn't gone on much longer when the ship sank. That was when the Swelkie was created, and it has whirled on ever since, for at that spot the great quern grinds on forever producing the salt for the sea, and the waters of the Pentland Firth pour eternally through the hole in Mysing's Grotte.

Early in the nineteenth century "The Swelkie" swallowed up a boat and the seven men of Freswick who manned her. She was a new boat bought in Stromness in Orkney and they were taking her home.

All went well till the fair winds died as they set course to cross the Firth. The moon was new and a strong ebb was pulling them westward where the Swelkie swirled and boiled. With no wind for the sails to draw they lowered them and bent their backs to the oars.

The Stroma folk assembled on the shore saw their danger. There were pilots among them who shouted and signalled to the hapless mariners to go south and wait for the tide to turn. But the crew appeared not to understand and on they came, till they were in the pull of the whirlpool and their boat would not respond to helm or oar. The Stroma folk shouted and the women screamed as the boat plunged on to her doom. The whirpool clutched her, spun her round and round. It had been believed among seafaring people that the Swelkie would be appeased if the boat's gear and the men's clothing were tossed into it. The victims surely remembered this theory for they threw all they had, including their garments, into the vortex. "The Swelkie" did not accept their offering, but mercilessly sucked them and everything they had down, down into the depths. Nothing from this disaster was ever cast up on the shore.

We were to see ships foolhardy enough to enter the flood tide at too steep an angle, roll and swing and very nearly capsize. An old coal burning steamer, caught between Stroma and South Ronaldsay when the ebb tide came into force, steamed at full power, black smoke belching from her funnel, for six hours and when at last the tide turned she had been carried back two or three miles.

So much for the behaviour of the tides, explained to me at a much later date by Mr James Allan, one of our Occasional Keepers.

Meantime, on that summer's day in 1955, we were introduced into the ready-made community of a lighthouse station, and began our life as islanders on the island in the tide.

Chapter Three

THE very next day the first of our many, many lodgers arrived. He was one of the engineers of the Lighthouse Board, Mr James Logie. When one is at last free to live with one's very own special person one rather resents having that long sought-for privacy intruded upon. However, part and parcel of our new life was that of playing host to a fairly steady stream of artificers from Edinburgh, as well as supernumeraries sent for training and keepers sent from other stations to do temporary stints of duty.

Mr Logie was accompanied by a gold-braided District Superintendent, Mr Macmillan, who had come to carry out the annual inspection of the station. Mr Macmillan lodged in the Principal Keeper's house, the sitting room being given over to him, as was the tradition. The Principal's wife was expected to serve his meals to him in solitary splendour in the sitting room. There were even dishes provided from which he was to eat. Judging by the size of the plates, ashets and tureens he was expected to devour quite gargantuan meals.

As soon as James Logie changed into his working clothes he quietly performed perhaps his most dangerous task. He climbed to the very top of the dome that capped the lighthouse tower and greased the weather-vane about sixty feet from earth.

I don't remember how I came to know of this feat, which must have taken considerable courage, for Mr Logie never mentioned it. When I knew of it, and spoke of it to him, expressing my admiration of his bravery, he only said, "I always do it first thing".

The rest of his stay he overhauled the engines that drove the foghorn on the cliff-top a few yards from the station's back gate.

The only times I had heard a foghorn was when visiting Jimmy's home in Deerness. Then the horn on the island of Copinsay, about three miles distant over the sea, would moan mournfully through the mist. On such occasions the thought had occurred to me that most likely I was going to find such a sound at close quarters very trying. I dreaded it causing headaches from which I suffered quite frequently.

However, on Stroma, early on, I had what I call "a mental click" about the horn. I thought "When the horn blows the lightkeepers are performing one of the most important parts of their job." Maybe I'd have become used to the horn anyhow and not minded it in time, but after formulating my thoughts about it, its blasts never bothered me in the slightest nor did it give me headaches. Indeed, the foghorn blowing just outside the station wall with a background of engine noise lost all the eerie quality I had associated with the Copinsay one, which I had heard only from a distance.

The red foghorn on Stroma protruded from a little

concrete building set on top of a high, white tower, the horn itself reminding one of those old-fashioned gramophone horns. Inside the little building on top of the tower was the clockwork mechanism, that controlled the "two blasts of three seconds each in quick succession every minute".

In the engine room attached to the base of the lighthouse tower there were three "Atlantic" petrol/paraffin engines. These, working two at a time, drove air compressors which pumped air into five, huge cylindrical, metal tanks. When the air reached twenty-four lb pressure, a valve was opened, and the air rushed through a large pipe into a second set of tanks in the base of the horn's tower.

The engines would roar into life. Then, with a great "Whoosh", the air would rush into the foghorn's "lungs", and out of the huge, red horn would issue two loud bellows.

While Mr Logie conducted the overhaul of all machinery, Mr Macmillan inspected. It was hinted that besides checking the fabric of the houses this official also made note of how well the housekeeping was being carried out. I saw several District Superintendents at work, but none of them made me aware that they had any interest in my housekeeping prowess.

Perhaps inspection of housekeeping was necessary in some cases. The story goes that one bachelor lightkeeper used to make enough porridge at one boiling to last him a week. This he stored in a drawer — cutting off the required slab each day. According to a guide I heard one summer in the cottage of Hugh Miller, the nineteenth-century geologist, this used to be an accepted way of preparing, storing and serving porridge in Scotland. Be that as it may, when the aforementioned lightkeeper's house was taken over by a new family they tried in vain for some time to track down the source of a horrible stench that persisted through the house. At last it was found — a very old lobster on top of a wardrobe!

Mr Logie, the engineer, was an elderly, bald gentleman with a long, lugubrious face and stomach trouble. Poor man, he had to endure many a cooking experiment while in my care. One of the worst was when I chose "Eggs in Snow" from a book entitled *101 Ways to Cook Eggs*, given me by my mother-in-law. You beat up the whites, spread them out in a pie dish, and made indentations in the white foam into which you plopped the yolks and covered them over with the white. The dish was then put in the oven for an unspecified time — and that was my undoing. Not endowed with much common sense, I had no idea how long to leave the dish in the oven, and so Jimmy and Mr Logie supped raw eggs nobly and uncomplainingly that tea-time. Mr Logie must have escaped more gratefully than ever that evening into his favourite world of the "wild west". His life's ambition was to visit the Grand Canyon. I wonder if he ever achieved it.

For cooking we had two stoves. One was a heavy, black, iron, coal-burning "Victoress", and the other a "Valor" paraffin stove with two burners, and for an oven, a tin cabinet to set on top of one burner. A round, glass tank fixed to one side held the paraffin.

It was on the Valor that I experimented with my brand new pressure pot. I was quite nervous about using it. A friend, seeing it among our wedding presents, said "Oh good, a pressure pot. It'll spit at you", and that remark stuck uneasily in my mind. To begin with I used to check that Jimmy was within calling distance before using it, and set a chair between me and the stove.

Only once did I bake a cake in it. The instructions were to dry the cake out in the oven after cooking in the pressure pot. Maybe I didn't leave it in the oven long enough, for one guest, on his second helping, beamed across the table at me, and said "Margaret, this cake is delicious, just the way I like it — just that little bit raw."

Heating of water, boiling and stewing I did on my "Victoress". The pots and pans provided were made of cast-iron. I, being a seven stone weakling, needed both hands to heave them about. The "Victoress" had to be black-leaded frequently — a messy job. I dressed up for it like some bandit — aproned, with a scarf over my hair and another over my nose and mouth. Its chimney was cleaned annually by Jimmy. He pushed down it a chimney brush on a rope weighted by a steel ball, and dragged the contraption up and down with great rumblings and clouds of soot until he decided the chimney was clean.

I remember when I was a small child being taken to visit a relative, who had some sort of stove with bars or ribs in front. Fascinated, I watched her push the poker between the ribs and draw it up and down to clear out the grey ash, and when I returned home I spent many happy hours poking with a stick between the ribs of a wooden kitchen chair. Now I had a real ribbed front fire to myself, and poking between the ribs never palled.

The whole body of the "Victoress" became hot, and the tilley lamp gave heat, as well as soft, pleasant-smelling light, so our kitchen was a lovely, warm room.

Once a week we heated water in zinc pails, placed our tin bungalow bath in front of the stove, and had a bath. Only in summer did we light the great, stone boiler in the wash-house and fill the proper bath out there. Though the wash-house became quite warm and steamy, a bath there was not nearly as nice as one in front of the fire in the kitchen.

I did all my baking and roasting in the tin cabinet of the "Valor" cooker, for the Victoress's oven was cracked and soot fell down in it. I found the ventilated tin box to be a most splendid oven. I used an oven thermometer and found I could control the temperature adequately. Every morning, Jimmy carried its glass tank to the oil store and there filled it with paraffin out of the enormous grey tanks with their gleaming brass taps and well burnished drip trays. Then I'd concoct Meat and Vegetable Pie or Baked Mince or Baked Meat Souffle. These were served with our own potatoes, carrots, turnips and cabbages from our allotted, walled-in plot down beside the shore near the North End Pier. Here we also grew lettuces for summer salads.

This "planticru" was an interesting garden in which to work. Indeed often too interesting for much progress to be made. I remember a typical afternoon when a squadron of oyster-catchers rested on the rocks, brilliant orange bills tucked into sooty black backs, one pink leg drawn up out of sight. Then, surely thinking of tea, one by one they raised their heads, revealing scarlet eyes, stretched out behind the bent pink legs, over which their black and white wings expanded skirt-like, so that their poise reminded one of ballerinas. Then on with the business of finding tea. They "stalked" their shelled prey over the weedy rocks and at the sea's edge. There would be a pause, as though listening and observing, a little run forward and then a long, orange bill pounced, poked and prized out the victim. A gannet sat swilling about on the sea. They didn't usually stay by the island, so we wondered if anything was wrong with it.

To return to our eating habits, we always had a pudding — such dishes as Queen of Puddings, Sun-maid Raisin Bread Pudding or Butterscotch Pie. All economical, nourishing, filling and fattening foods.

From an old diary I see I baked on Mondays and Thursdays. "Slimming" and "dieting" were not words in common use in those days. When I think of our meals I marvel that we did not become round, fat dumplings.

My favourite recipe books were *The Dundee Cookery Book*,

to which I'd been introduced when having Domestic Science lessons in Kirkwall Grammar School, and *The Glasgow Cookery Book*, a wedding gift from a fellow teacher. I especially liked how, when it gave a measurement in spoonfuls, it meant level spoonfuls. I also used a copy of the *Scottish Women's Rural Institutes Cookery Book* — first published in 1928 — mine was the sixth edition of 1946 passed on by my mother-in-law. I obtained too the invaluable little Be-Ro book advertised on packets of Be-Ro self-raising flour. Just the other week Jimmy read from a newspaper that the Be-Ro firm are offering the prize of £1,000 for the oldest copy sent them. You may be sure I immediately looked out my coverless, dough-stained copy. Alas, it is only the twenty-first edition. Since they've been in production for sixty years Jimmy assured me my copy stood no chance.

Every baking session I would produce brown scones and white scones, something made with pastry, brown cakes and white cakes and biscuits. And, with the help of friends and neighbours, the tins would all be emptied by the next session.

Sometimes the white scones were dropped scones baked on a greased girdle; sometimes, flour bannocks on the heavy iron girdle sprinkled with flour. I only had grease-proof paper to wipe off the flour, which was not as romantic as my grandmother's little bunch of feathers, or "pens" as she called them.

Pastry might be represented by something savoury, like Sausage Rolls, or Egg and Bacon Pie, or something sweet such as Lemon Meringue Pie made with a fresh lemon and not, as I lazily do now, with a handy powder mix.

Brown scones were usually treacle ones, while brown cakes consisted of little Coburg Cakes, or a big Chocolate Spice Cake. I also made an eggless cake, though there certainly was no need for me to be parsimonious with eggs.

It had a breakfast cup of cold tea in it and we liked it very much. My white cakes could be Queen Cakes or what was called in the recipe book "Butterfly Cakes" which, Jimmy has insisted through the years, I always described at that time as "Angels on horseback". Maybe he's right, for they were wingéd cakes, but why on earth should I have invented such a name?

The first time one visitor tasted and expressed enjoyment of one of my attempts at biscuits, which I explained were called "Melting Moments", the result was amazing. "My goodness, I've forgotten to put the cats out," he exclaimed. Then added, with a wry smile, "Bet when I get home there'll be plenty of melting moments."

Ingredients were no problem, for Jimmy, knowledgeable about lighthouse life, advised keeping at least a month's stock of non-perishable foodstuffs, just in case the weather prevented the boat crossing.

Though we had an income of about £7 per week we managed to gradually stock the walk-in cupboard so that it resembled a little shop. There were bags of flour, sugar, lentils, beans and peas. There were tins of syrup, treacle, meats, fruits, baking powder, cream of tartar, and bicarbonate of soda. There were drums of salt, pepper, ginger, mixed spice and cinnamon. There were packets of dried fruit, custard powder, cornflour and tea. We usually had a round red ball of Edam cheese. Jars of marmalade, jams, beetroot and coffee also had their place. We bought our biscuits by the tin.

At that time a bag of flour cost 1s. 7½d., a bag of sugar 1s. 5d., half a pound of margarine 8d. and a tin of Nescafé 3s. 6d. A brown loaf cost 5d., a milk loaf 6d. and a plain loaf 9½d. To my regret I never tried to make bread. Mrs Lamont once gave me a tin of dried yeast, but our supply boat was never so long overdue that we missed having bread. I made scones instead. One Principal's wife did experiment once, and produced several little loaves which we all tasted.

Sometimes our Occasional Keeper, James Allen, would present us with a freshly caught fish hooked by "ripper". I didn't like the sound of the implement. "The ripper" was a length of polished lead with rows of fish hooks attached. It sounded such a cruel, violent object to use, but, come to think of it, the most refined and beautiful of fishing flies have the same end result.

Nor did I enjoy putting the occasional gift of a lobster to its death. I used to insist that the giver held on to the crustacean — I was terrified of their powerful, snapping claws — until I'd brought a large pot of water to the boil. The giver had then to plunge the creature headfirst into the pot so that the unbearable scrabbling against the pot lid in a last desperate effort to live was as short as possible. One lobster giver, holding his gift as per my instructions, put a whole box of matches between the lobster's claw. Box and contents were immediately pulverised. I feared a conflagration.

Eggs we had in abundance. The hens we inherited when Donald, our First Assistant, was posted and later those we bought as fertilised eggs and incubated under "Old White" — one of Donald's veterans — kept us supplied in plenty. I preserved the excess eggs in a preservative called "Oteg", a thick liquid into which you dipped each egg, making sure it was completely covered with the waxy liquid. The eggs were then allowed to dry and could be stored in boxes. "Oteg" was excellent stuff, and we never had a bad egg.

Our hens inhabited a little stone building near the cliff edge. The cliffs nearby were low, and at places level with the rock-slabbed beach. Every day the hens would make a journey along the beach to a cove which I named "Hen's Bay". When Mr William Bremner, an old island friend, named for me all the parts of the island, I found this cove was known as "Goosgoe". Did somebody at some time have geese that took the same outing as our hens, or was it a haunt of wild geese?

Donald kept his hens in an empty cottage on top of the little heather-covered hill in front of the station. Empty cottages were plentiful in Stroma. Depopulation had started about the time of the 1914-18 war, and had continued through the years so that when we arrived there were only about eighty people on the island where in 1914 there had been 300. Islanders said that when 300 people were there the island had really suffered from overpopulation. Some recalled seeing cows tethered at the roadsides to obtain grazing, and even the grass growing in rock crevices had to be used.

I began to look for reasons why the people were uprooting themselves like this, and had been doing so over quite a long period.

It seemed that in the first place the First World War had had an unsettling effect, taking people away from the island and perhaps showing them easier ways of living.

At a much later date had come Education Acts, making it necessary or possible, however one looked at the arrangement, for the young to go to the mainland for more advanced schooling. Many did not return. Further afield were opportunities to follow trades and professions, and to lead fuller social lives than was possible in a small island community of crofter/fishermen. Parents left to be nearer their families.

Older people with no member of their household able to handle boats or take part in the landing and transporting of the annual boat-load of coal felt at a disadvantage.

In 1955 a project was afoot which, it was hoped, would stop the depopulation. This was the building of a new harbour in which boats would be able to lie afloat safely throughout all weathers. Up to this time boats had had to be hauled out of the water and beached at every hint of bad weather.

The harbour was to cost £30,000.

Islanders were employed under the supervision of an engineer and supplemented by a diver. I did not meet the diver, but Jimmy did before I joined him on the island.

The diver, like Donald the First Assistant, came from the Western Isles. One evening the former arrived at the light-house to pay Donald a visit, but Donald was not at home. Jimmy therefore invited him into our house to have a cup of tea and wait until Donald returned.

In our kitchen/living room Jimmy had erected book-shelves which were well-stocked with our joint libraries. To find a mutual conversational topic, Jimmy asked the diver what kind of books he read.

"I read only one book," was the reply.

"And what's that?" asked Jimmy.

" *The Bible.* "

From then on he spent the entire evening laying forth about what a rotter he'd been till he'd been converted to Christianity, and preached on and on at Jimmy.

At long last Donald arrived. Jimmy provided him with tea too, but from that time on Donald and the diver carried on their conversation exclusively in Gaelic. Jimmy did rather wonder what was being discussed — perhaps him?

The coming of a proper harbour, alas, did not quell the flood of depopulation. In some cases it hastened it, for people working at its construction made regular wages that helped them to buy houses in Caithness.

Talking to Jimmy one day about the depopulation I unwittingly told him a most peculiar fib. "D'you know," said I, "Mr Polson, who owns the island, makes Thermos flasks in Yorkshire?"

"Really?" said Jimmy in a puzzled tone. "I always

understood he was called Hoyland and that he manufactured umbrella frames."

At once I realised that this was so. Why I should have thought of Thermos flasks and Polson, I've no idea. The only time I saw the name Polson was on the cornflour packet.

Mr Hoyland must have been a very unhappy person at that time for as each house was vacated he discovered that he had to pay compensation to its owner. He owned the land. The home owners had improved his sites by building houses on them. He had bought Stroma in 1946 for about £4,000.

Vainly, and to the islanders great indignation, he tried to sell the island by advertising it in West German newspapers, and even contemplated allowing an American TV quiz show to offer it as a prize. The Stroma folk did not want a foreign owner.

They were not alone in their consternation. Important people in the Foreign Office, the Admiralty and Scottish Office got together to discuss the matter.

Stroma was in a strategic position. It was close to the naval anchorage of Scapa Flow and was also near South Uist in the west, where the Government intended setting up a top secret rocket missile site.

The Whitehall officials decided that Mr Hoyland was free to sell Stroma to anybody anywhere in the world. However, the island would continue to be part of Her Majesty's domain, and, under the Aliens Restrictions Act, if a foreign purchaser proved to be unsuitable in the eyes of the Foreign Office, they could forbid him from setting foot on his purchase.

Incidentally, this was not the first time Stroma had been of strategic importance. When Orkney and Caithness were part of the same earldom, the Norse earls used to appoint a governor to reside in Stroma, and no doubt keep them informed of events in their lands in nearby Caithness.

On one occasion we know of, such an official, Arnilot by name, proved his worth. A marauding band of High-landers invaded Caithness and plundered as far north as Canisbay. The governor on Stroma promptly sent word to the Earl in Orkney who at once crossed the Firth. He encountered the invaders near Duncansby Head, defeated them, and forced them to give up all their loot.

Chapter Four

NEARLY every day somebody from the lighthouse went up the road, a bumpy, stony, holey track that crossed the middle of the island from north to south. Always, whoever was going would call in at each house door, "I'm away up the road. Can I get you anything?"

And you felt a little thrill of excitement for there might be mail waiting at the Post Office if a boat had been across to the mainland.

"Up the road" as well as taking you to the Post Office, passed the only shop and solitary telephone booth. The telephone kiosk was beside the church gate. It was a radio telephone, and when you used it you had to wait some minutes until it switched itself on, and was ready to transmit.

This telephone had only been installed in 1953. Up till

1935 Stroma folk had to send urgent messages to the main-land by signalling with a lamp when the weather was too bad for a boat to cross. People on the mainland wanting to contact the island urgently had either to lay a sheet over a certain peat-stack or light a bonfire on the beach. This did not always work. In the School Log of 1872 the teacher complained, "Detained on the mainland. Could get no boat from the Island across for me." Was he storm-bound or did everybody feel a school holiday was called for? In 1935 a radio phonogram link was put in.

We too were once "detained on the mainland", but looking at the unleashed Sound rampaging and roaring, whipped into a fury by the remorseless howling wind, we knew no amount of phoning would bring a boat across for us.

"They're fairly dancin' out there to-night," quipped the proprietor of the John o' Groats hotel, referring to an article I'd written for *The Scots Magazine*, in which I described the Firth as a stage and the waves as dancers.

I was disappointed to discover that the hotel had nothing to do with the famous octagonal house of John de Groat. I say famous, but alas James Calder, the Caithness historian, doesn't believe the story about it at all. The story goes that when John invited seven relatives to meet him in his house by the shores of the Pentland Firth they all fell out as to who should have precedence in coming through the door, and who should sit at the top of the table. John poured oil on the troubled waters, by reminding them how they had prospered since coming from their native land of Holland to Scotland, and asked them to go in peace and not molest each other, bearing in mind that they were kith and kin. He promised that when they gathered the following year he'd have solved the problem of precedence.

So he built a house with eight doors and windows and

furnished it with an octagonal oak table. When the party arrived, he showed each man to his own door, and to the head of the table.

However, through the centuries, travellers to these parts made no mention of this unusual building. In 1698 the Rev John Brand, Commissioner of the General Assembly, lived in the northernmost house in Scotland, which was at that date an inn kept by John Grot, but there is no word of the building itself being in any way remarkable.

A writer of 1769 refers to "the famous house called John o' Groat's", but doesn't give reasons for its fame.

Perhaps Calder is right and there never was an octagonal John o' Groat's house.

Anyhow I always think warmly of that northern corner, for Jimmy and I spent the most delightful weekend in the John o' Groat's hotel. The peat fire blazed in the lounge which we had to ourselves, and we sat in great comfort and enjoyed the books we'd newly bought in Wick. I can't remember what Jimmy had, but I had D H Lawrence's letters — the sight of which always recalls for me that unscheduled, luxurious little holiday.

There was no connection between the radio telephone in the kiosk and the telephone at the lighthouse. The latter communicated only with Stroma Post Office. So, when the teacher's husband, Mr Ted Thomson, found the eggs beginning to hatch in a green plover's nest which he knew Jimmy had photographed previously, and was hoping to photograph again during and after hatching, he summoned Jimmy and camera to the scene by phoning John o' Groat's Post Office by radio telephone, and asking them to pass the message back to Stroma Post Office, who could then let Jimmy know by phoning the lighthouse.

We got our pictures.

The Post Office was first established in Stroma in 1879 when the population was over 200. The Postmaster was paid £7 5s. a year, and the letter deliverer 1s. weekly plus 5s. for ferrying mails over from Huna.

Seventy five years later, when the population had fallen to about eighty, the mail contractor was paid £432 for a three day a week crossing, and the Postmaster's salary had risen to £230. It was estimated that the cost of carrying each letter to the island had risen to 1s. 7d.

Both Post Office and shop were enjoyable to visit. Mr Donald Wares presided pleasantly at the Post Office. Miss Jessie Smith and Mr John Sinclair ran the branch of the Scottish Wholesale Co-operative Society cheerfully and efficiently.

Their stock was almost as multifarious as that of our present day supermarkets. They sold everything from paraffin, torch batteries and scouring powder, aptly named "Rubitof", to tins of sweets, chocolate biscuits and crimped, nylon socks.

I only once nearly stumped them. That was when I asked for a bottle brush, "to scrub out the milk bottles," I explained.

"Och, just tie a rag on the end of a stick," advised Jessie. I did, and it worked.

Fellow customers related anecdotes from the past, and joked together, while one octogenarian entertained the company by doing "the splits".

When Jimmy first arrived he aroused considerable interest once in the shop, by asking where he could find James Robertson.

"James Robertson?" Nobody knew anyone of that name.

"I was on Rattray with his nephew George Robertson," Jimmy explained. "He told me to look him up."

This brought an immediate response from the assembled company.

"Och, you mean 'Dooble'," they cried in unison. James

51

Robertson indeed — he was never known as anything but "Dooble" in Stroma.

Jessie and John did not venture into the fields of fashion or furniture. For such items we had to turn to "catalogue shopping".

Jimmy and I soon discovered that two fireside chairs were not enough. The lighthouse authorities provided only hard, upright, wooden chairs, and though I fitted them out with cushions, they were not suitable for long or relaxed sitting.

But there in our large, glossy catalogues from mail order firms were comfortable chairs and neat chests of drawers, another item for which we soon found a need.

Though my most usual garb for life on Stroma was a pair of slacks, and oilskin, jacket or duffle coat, wellington boots or stout walking shoes, I shudder to think how much money I squandered on garments that looked so smart on the svelte models in catalogues. Of course, when we visited or went to church we dressed up. Jimmy's civilian clothes were sports jackets and flannels. I used to change into a dress for the evenings, even when staying at home, so there was some excuse for some of the buys. I knitted our jerseys and sewed some of my dresses on my sewing machine which I'd bought for my bottom drawer.

Most tempting of all for us were the book publishers' catalogues. Neither Jimmy nor I could resist buying books, so many a list went across the Sound. And then there was the excitement and fun of opening all the interesting parcels.

Jimmy had weekly reading material sent to him — *Practical Mechanics*, *Practical Motorist* and *The Woodworker*. We took the *Scots Magazine*. I took *Woman* out of which I once bought a ready-cut-out dress in poppy-coloured silky material and made it up. It was my favourite for a long time. I also collected vast numbers of their articles for embroidery, thinking I'd be sure to get them all done. I've passed on a boxful to my daughter, in the hope she'll succeed where I failed.

But the books were the most exciting parcels. *Seal Morning* by Rowena Farre we both enjoyed immensely. How let down I felt when years later I read it was only a fictitious story! *The Houses in Between* by Howard Spring interested Jimmy and me, as did that enchanting book, *Island Years* by Fraser Darling.

Jimmy liked stronger meat than I, and he went for *Green Hell*, a book about exploration in the Amazon jungles, *Seven Years in Tibet* and *Steamboat Gothic*. I found Mrs Robert Henrey's style to my taste in her autobiographical works — *The Little Madeleine and Madeleine Grown up*. I think it was from the second-hand department of Thins of Edinburgh that we procured H G Wells' *Experiment in Autobiography*. I must say I'm philistine enough to prefer factual, real-life stories to the perhaps higher art form of the novel.

I don't think catalogue shopping would have been as necessary in earlier days on Stroma.

There were once four shops on the island, and from about 1910 to the Great War, and for a few years after 1918, Stroma was served weekly, through the summer months, by "The Floating Shops", a little fleet of sailing smacks from Orkney.

It was when my grandmother came to visit us that I first heard of "The Floating Shops". My grandmother and Mr James Allan, the older of our two Occasional Keepers, were reminiscing about their youth, when my grand-mother amazed me by remarking, "I used to pack boxes of boots for the floating shops. They used to come here."

Mr Allan replied that they had, and it had been a great day when the floating shops arrived. I then proceeded to question them, for I wanted to know more about this unusual phenomenon — a floating shop.

It was a wide-awake Kirkwall merchant who conceived the idea of fitting out as shops a little fleet of sailing smacks. Looking from Kirkwall in any direction, this must have seemed an obvious course to take. Islands of possible customers lay all around him. The islands of Shetland, the North and South Isles of Orkney, and Stroma, the only island of the county of Caithness, were eventually served at Robert Garden's counters, brought regularly to them by *Star of Bethlehem*, *Summer Cloud*, *Gleaner*, *Star of Hope*, and *Endeavour*.

The boat I know about is the *Star of Hope*, which called once a fortnight, all through the summer months, at the north end of Stroma. The *Endeavour* came to the south side of the island each alternate week, but as Mr Allan's home was no distance from the north end pier, it was the *Star of Hope* he knew best, and described to me.

At the sight of her white sails approaching from Orkney, the word was passed round. "The floating shop's coming!" was the signal for various preparations to be made, for she came not only to sell but to buy.

The womenfolk gathered eggs into white enamel pails and lidded baskets. Fishermen set about preparing what they called "the wet fish". At this time of year, when the fish were plentiful, and the market limited for disposing of fresh catches, a method of pickling was used.

On the boats' return from sea, possibly late in the evenings, the fish were cleaned, split, boned, and washed in fresh water. Then, after being allowed to drip for a few minutes, they were laid, layer about with salt, in a barrel. In about three days' time the fish were floating in salt pickle.

When the floating shop was sighted the fish were swished about in the pickle to remove any sliminess, piled up, covered with canvas, and a large stone was placed on top to press out the water. Then, in barrows and baskets, they were taken to the store and loaded into the boats.

Boxes of lobsters were also put aboard, and, from as far as John o' Groat's and Mey on the Caithness coast, local boats brought their catch.

By the time the *Star of Hope* reached her anchorage at the north end, the pier there was crowded with people from every part of the island.

The fishermen, with their boat-loads for sale, were ready to go out to the ship. The other customers settled down to wait their turn to be ferried out, three or four at a time, in the floating shop's own small rowing boat.

The floating shop had a crew of three, and each man was in charge of a department. Nearest the bow of the ship was the grocer at his counter.

Along the bulkheads and sides of the ship were shelves on which the groceries were displayed. Bars of wood were nailed in front of the goods to prevent their tumbling off the shelves.

Midships there was kept the meal and feeding-stuffs. A large weighing machine stood in the centre, and sacks of flour, oatmeal, bere meal, bran and Indian corn were built up along the sides.

The least busy of the departments was nearest the stern — the drapery. The draper had his goods set out on a bench right round his domain, as well as on barred shelves and hanging on criss-cross lines above his head. When a lull came, and no one wanted a pair of boots, a roll of wall-paper, an overall or oilskin, it didn't mean he could relax. He was expected to jump on deck and deal with the incoming lobsters and fish.

He counted the lobsters, paid out 1s. or 1s. 2d. for each, and packed them in the ship's own boxes. These, when full, he dumped overboard to keep the supply fresh and alive until the ship was ready to leave.

The fish he weighed on deck, giving about 8s. to 10s. per

hundredweight, and then stacked them and covered them over with canvas.

The grocer bought in the dozens of eggs at 6d. per dozen, and packed them between layers of straw in large boxes. Part of his duties took him on deck too, for he was responsible for the casks of paraffin lashed there.

The three men must have had a hard-working five hours or so in their often hot, rather cramped premises. Frequently too, there was a strong rolling motion to endure — the cause of considerable discomfort to some of the women customers.

At the end of the day's business the hatches were closed, mainsail set, anchor heaved in, and foresail hoisted. Usually this was carried out as uneventfully as the putting up of shutters in a quiet street. On one occasion however this was not so.

As the *Star of Hope* lay at anchor the wind changed, and was beating hard on shore when she tried to leave. The man working the hand winch to heave the anchor aboard was suddenly knocked unconscious by a snapped pinion from the anchor windlass.

Fortunately the local boatmen, as was their custom, had stayed to help with the heaving of the anchor. The injured man was cared for, and then the little boats towed the ship round until her head was turned offshore and her sails able to catch the wind.

Stroma enjoyed this service from about 1910 to the Great War, and for a few years after 1918 it was resumed with engine-driven ships.

But as early as 1897, the girl who was to become my grandmother, filled huge wooden boxes with boots, bales of mens' shirting, wool, and the half-bleached cotton ladies used for making their underwear.

It must often have seemed a tiresome way to earn her weekly 6s. and realise the distant dream of a hat trimmed

56

with roses. Would it have lightened the task had she known she was helping to stock the Aladdin's cave of many another girl?

By comparison our shopping was very ordinary. Nobody would expect any great drama with a landbound shop, nor was there with ours, but on occasion a shopping expedition could contain at least one amusing episode.

One hot summer's day, Donald, Jimmy and I were returning home from the shop when we came upon a North End neighbour, "Old Andy", seated astride the ditch, his head shielded from the sun's rays by a white handkerchief knotted at each of its corners.

"Oi'm just weytin' for the rib," said Old Andy, pointing up the road behind with his walking stick.

Puzzled, we turned to see what he was pointing at. A plump, little woman bearing a bulky, message bag in each hand, was waddling down the road.

Donald began to laugh.

"Whit are ye laughin' at?" demanded Andy putting on a show of indignation. "She's called 'the rib' in the Good Book. It says He took the rib o' the man and from it made the woman."

By this time "the rib" had reached us, and with little ceremony shooed Andy homewards.

"I was chust thinking," said Donald with a twinkle in his eye, "Andy can't haf many ribs left. That's hiss third one."

Chapter Five

DONALD, our First Assistant, received a posting, and his place was taken by another bachelor, Johnny Thomson, a fellow Orcadian hailing from the most northerly island of Orkney — North Ronaldsay. All at once Jimmy was First Assistant, for he had been longer in the service than Johnny.

Mr Lamont, our Principal Keeper, took ill and had to be taken off the island. Suddenly Jimmy was in temporary charge of the station.

The Northern Lighthouse Board's promotion system was by stepping into "dead men's shoes". Being young and lacking in experience, we used to feel impatient that this was the only way to the top. Now, having experienced more of the ways of the world, we realise just how much more humane was the way of the Board, compared to the often grossly unfair race methods employed elsewhere. The older, more experienced men were rewarded with a position of responsibility, dignity and increased salary in due time. Failure in duty, misbehaviour, and especially committing the worst sin — that of letting the light stand — resulted, if not in dismissal, in being put down some steps in the climb to becoming Principal Lightkeeper.

The Lamont family all left Stroma while Mr Lamont was in hospital — all except Monty, their Shetland collie, who came to stay with us till their return.

Monty was a delightful, good natured dog. We grew to love him. I remember one occasion when his presence was of especial comfort to me.

I hadn't been feeling very well, and had taken two Codeine tablets — the only time I ever did that — and retired to bed. Jimmy was on watch from midnight to 3 am and during this time I suddenly woke up in the dark room. There on the side of the bed, back to me, sat a despondent man in a dark suit. "What's wrong, Jimmy?" I asked, stretching out my hand to click on a battery powered bedside light. With the light, the man vanished. Shaking, I made my way to the bell push to summon Jimmy down from the tower. He arrived as quickly as he could to find out what was wrong. I told my story. Jimmy sensibly reminded me of the tablets I'd taken, and put forward the theory that they'd given me a hallucination. He did his best to comfort and cheer me up ending with the bright idea that Monty should come through and stay beside me till the watch was changed.

Years later we told Mr William Bremner, an old Island friend, of this incident. He listened in silence, and then after a pause said wonderingly, "But it wasn't in your house that the fellow lived who threw himself off the tower." We'd never heard of this tragedy before.

Another rather strange experience took place in our sitting room.

59

One evening in that room a Supernumerary Keeper offered to take a photograph of us both together. At that time Jimmy was quite new to photography, and for some reason thought that if one used flash bulbs the room's lights had to be extinguished. The only light remaining was that of the dying embers of the coal fire. We posed — I in the chair, Jimmy on the arm. Jim Crowe, the young trainee, pressed the button and the flash failed to go off. The room light was again switched on, the bulb replaced in the flash mechanism, and once more plunged into darkness he clicked the shutter open. Again the flash failed. Once more the bulb was replaced, and on this third attempt the flash was operated successfully. I should like to have the results of all three trials reproduced here. Maybe somebody can explain the photographs produced on the first two attempts, in virtually complete darkness. The one resembled to Jimmy, floodlit spaghetti; to me, an entanglement of curled up fingers. The other consisted of one straight band of light with a bulge in the middle, reminiscent of x-rays of leg bones. We didn't know what to think.

Indeed, I wasn't long in Stroma before I was wondering what to think about all sorts of things. People often wish they had time to think, and that if they could go to some isolated spot they could do so to some effect. With this sort of desire goes the notion that alone in the quiet places one would automatically find peace of mind, wisdom — the answers to life's questions. It wasn't my experience.

I had been a fundamentalist Christian for many years, having been brought up in the doctrines and beliefs of the Plymouth Brethren, of which sect at the age of fifteen I became a baptised, believing member. Baptism I'd dreaded from before school age when I witnessed a relative called Auntie Maggie and her son Harry, whom I adored, being laid below the waves in the total immersion baptism

60

in the sea, carried out by the Brethren in Orkney. Without fail I burst into tears whenever visiting evangelists, on checking with my father that I was "saved", turned to me, too shy and unsure of my spiritual situation to speak for myself, and said kindly but firmly, "Well she knows the next step." For years the fear of this ordeal to come haunted me, but in the end I had to surrender and comply with my society's mores.

As the years passed and the company of young people, who during the war had been stationed in Orkney and had attended the meetings of the Brethren and the Salvation Army with me, was withdrawn, I found my lonely existence as an attender of those religious bodies beyond enduring.

I began attending the Church of Scotland where a Youth Fellowship was organised. There I enjoyed associating once again with people of my own age. I also decided that the negative outlook on taking part in what the Brethren regarded as worldly pursuits, such as dancing and drama, was not for me. I wished to do some living while I had the chance. Fellow students during my period of teacher training in Edinburgh, who held the same Christian beliefs as I, did not consider it sinful to dance or attend the theatre or cinema, which I had been told as a child was "the devil's house".

By the time I met Jimmy, fell in love with him and married him, ex-friends of the Brethren persuasion were writing me to say rather threateningly that perhaps I thought I was managing to run away from my Brethren family and background, but they could assure me I wouldn't manage to escape "the Lord".

At that point I had no intention of escaping from anybody. Despite the remarks of the minister who was our religious instructor at College, that there were pillars under the sea of Galilee by which Jesus walked "on the

61

water", and that in all probability Jesus was the illegitimate child of a Roman soldier, I still believed that Jesus was God's Son and our Saviour and that the Bible was true and the Word by which God spoke to us.

I now danced and took part in amateur drama, but neither drank, smoked nor indulged in pre-marital sex — the "sins" such activities were likely to lead to in Brethren eyes. One member of "the meeting", as the Brethren described themselves, presented me with a pile of leaflets entitled *The Sin of Dancing* — *of Smoking* and so on.

However, on Stroma, Jimmy, before I arrived, had become friends with the teacher and her husband, Mr Edward Thomson, a retired electrical and mechanical engineer. Mr T, as we privately and affectionately called him, was a tall, distinguished looking, silver-haired man, with dark eyes always lit with a twinkle of humour — sometimes mischievous humour. He was widely read, well-travelled, well-educated, a far cleverer, more experienced and worldly wise person than I.

He and Jimmy discussed all sorts of topics, from those of a practical nature such as engine maintenance and clock-making and mending, which Mr T did skilfully, to philosophy and religion.

He told us how he had ambled on at school, making little effort, but getting by, until, one day in his teens, while idly watching a large lorry backing in a street, he had a sudden revelation — "the light on the road to Damascus", he said with a chuckle. All at once it came to him that his life was in his own hands. That nobody could do anything about his future but himself. From then on he set about making the most of his education and prepared himself for his future career, that of a mechanical and electrical engineer. Many parents and teachers would no doubt wish this sort of experience took place more frequently.

My fundamentalist evangelical beliefs were soon

scotched. I could not argue successfully in their defence. They seemed naive, half-baked and ridiculous.

Mr T was a member of the Church of Scotland just because he thought the power of organised religion was the only means of keeping discipline among people.

He used to conclude some of my weak protestations with a quote from one of his aunts, "The Bible is like a fiddle, you can play any tune you like on it," and I had to admit this seemed so when one saw the varying interpretations made of it.

As for an after-life — what a monstrous idea — when the brain cells ceased to function that was the end.

Mrs T stuck nobly to her conventional Church of Scotland convictions, ending all discussion by saying "With God everything is possible," and refusing to be shaken.

Mr T would grin impishly and say, "Jimmy won't be in Heaven with you." Common sense seemed on his side. I hadn't had any great spiritual experiences to convince me about anything, and so many cleverer people than I disagreed profoundly and reasonably with what I had always accepted unquestioningly before. I became a "don't know", still on the side of the angels, but with an open, unresolved mind.

My Salvationist grandmother, I suspect feeling a little guilty when picnicking on Stroma on a Sunday instead of attending her Salvation Army services, would say rather defensively, "Of course you can worship God out in the world He created, just as well as in a kirk or a hall."

But out in the natural world I discovered many facts that made it impossible for me to follow this adage. The great skua showed no mercy to the kittiwake it held under the water till the victim drowned, and then left it like so much flotsam, so that one couldn't explain need for food as its motive. The great blackbacked gulls plucked the eyes out

63

of the sheep who'd rolled helplessly on their backs. The sheep were already dead when we saw them, so maybe the gulls were just making use of a no longer needed part which to them was a delicacy. I hope so. The ravens robbed the guillemots of their eggs. They lay scattered over the cliff-tops in their dozens — cracked, empty shells. In the natural world there was little sign of loving kindness or tender mercy.

What to make of it all? I didn't know, I still don't.

The coming of a Church of Scotland lay preacher or missionary did nothing to change my new found agnosticism. Indeed his behaviour if anything hardened it. He'd scarcely arrived before he was trying to persuade a most outraged Mr T to be anointed with oil for the common cold. He hardly endeared himself to us when he announced that you could draw a line at Inverness, and anything north of that he inferred wasn't up to much. He disapproved thoroughly of our Moffat translation of the Bible. Moffat, in his estimation, had not been a Christian. Jimmy suggested that surely it was his ability as a linguist that mattered. Moffat, it was pointed out, said in (I think) Isaiah "a King", while the King James VI translation said, "the King". Moffat was not to be countenanced.

This gentleman was an ex-Pentecostal Church member from Glasgow. He stated that the Church of Scotland was dead, and he'd joined in order to resuscitate it. Soon he was complaining that unlike Glaswegians, who apparently confessed freely on the streets that they were sinners, Caithness people would admit to no such thing.

We went to his few first services, for we thought that perhaps a resident preacher and regularly opened church would re-light a community spirit on the island, and put a stop to the continual depopulation.

However, it wasn't long till the congregation very nearly consisted of the "two or three gathered together", one of

64

whom I knew attended because he thought it was good for people to have a reason for dressing up once a week.

The church closed, and I, with my ministerially frowned upon lipstick and short hair-style, continued to wonder and ponder unaided, and to little avail.

Chapter Six

I NEVER felt lonely on Stroma, not even when the population consisted of one family of four and the lighthouse staff. Most important of all I had the company of the person with whom I most liked to be.

Jimmy — kind, considerate, and with a lively mind that took interest in many, many things, was the ideal companion. I always preferred his telling me of events, contents of books and so on to experiencing directly myself, and I still do.

When "the whowl place shook i' the winter-time", we would venture out — Jimmy helping me against the strong, buffeting wind — and look over the half size iron back gate — the only viewing point in the sturdy high wall that protected the station on the seaward sides. Great, grey-green billows would rush shorewards to dash themselves in whote foam over the rocks. Herring gulls would hang suspended in the grey clouded sky as though being restrained by an invisible hand, while shags would beat their black winged way low over the heaving water.

Sometimes a ship would venture past, one minute bucked high on the back of a billow, the next floundering almost out of sight in the trough of the wave, tossed about like a child's plaything.

Spray swept over the island like hazy sheets of salt rain. Windows were bleared with salt and brass knobs were sticky to the touch.

Usually on such a day we were cut off physically from the rest of the world. Reading one of Robert Morley's delightful books, I came on a good description of such times — "Recovery Days". Mr Morley asks if no one has ever thought of a calendar on which certain days every year are not recorded. He suggests they would not count as time, but be days in which the world could catch up with itself. Well, during a storm on Stroma, we very nearly achieved such an ideal.

When Jimmy was free we'd happily tune in to the BBC on our battery operated radio, and get on, while we listened, with marquetry, knitting and sewing. I tried always to listen to *Woman's Hour*, and *Mrs Dale's Diary* couldn't be missed. Together, we enjoyed a serialised *Cranford*, plays like *The Chiltern Hundreds*, *Desert Island Discs*, and I see from an old diary we enthused over *Renaissance*, a programme about Scottish literature in which a bevy of famous writers took part — Neil Gunn, Compton Mackenzie, Eric Linklater, James Burke, George Blake, Dr Edwin Muir and his wife Willa. A programme after which I wrote a synopsis of its contents, so impressed had we been, was *Seven Years Solitary*, the story of Dr Edith Bone's imprisonment in Hungary. I ended by saying "I'd never have dreamed that the human spirit was capable of such heights of fortitude and endurance."

During one spell of bad weather I wrote my first effort for publication, a letter to *Woman* in which I told of the catching up with correspondence, the reading of books because no new reading matter was arriving to distract, and the trying out of recipes with what was most plentiful in the store-cupboard, for no boat could cross with fresh provisions.

They published my letter and paid me a guinea:

Cut off

My island home is separated from the well-known John o' Groats by a three-mile stretch of moody water. Frequently its moods are so bad that the motor boat can't cross to the mainland for mail and provisions. Then, for maybe a week, the bustling world carries on without actual contact from us.
At this time I get busy with my pen and marvel how quickly my pile of letters to be answered dwindles. And as there are no fresh newspapers to read, at last I get the chance to take that favourite book from the shelf. Each meal becomes a surprise as I invent dishes and try out new recipes with the remaining stores.
Provided it's not too long and the store cupboard's well stocked, the calm in the storm is most enjoyable.
– Mrs T A (Stroma, Caithness).

Reply

How we envy you your seclusion on occasions, Mrs T A, especially when we get caught in rush-hour traffic or have to suffer the never-ceasing strains from neighbouring wirelesses. But we also consider that life must be hard and lonely for you at times. In future we'll pay far more attention to the radio forecasts of bad weather in the Caithness area, and think of you writing all those letters, with maybe one addressed to us.

"My writing career has started — what ho," wrote I conceitedly in my diary. William Bremner meanwhile thoroughly mystified Johnny, our Second Assistant, by enquiring of him, "Do you take *Woman*?" Johnny could not think why he'd been asked such an unmanly question. We fortunately could enlighten him and put his mind at rest.

Though nobody from the rest of the island would venture down to us on our northerly tip in such weather, we could still count on the company of our lighthouse neighbours.

The Lamont family did not return, as Mr Lamont's health forced him to resign.

They were replaced with a new Principal Keeper, Mr Alastair Hislop and his wife. Often we invited them and Johnny, the Second Assistant, in for the evening, and they always returned hospitality.

Our entertainment of guests took the form of listening to records — such favourites as John McCormack singing "I'll walk beside you", Father Sydney MacEwan's Irish songs and the Scottish tenor, Kenneth McKellar praising "Fair Rothesay Bay". We were also quite up to date, according to us, with Eartha Kitt's "Just an old fashioned girl" and her m-millionaire, and "Under the Bridges of Paris", which had been all the rage when we were on our honeymoon. Neither of us was very musical. Jimmy claims he'll stand to attention just as readily for "Auld Lang Syne" as "God Save the Queen". He bought the mechanical part of a record player and built it into a chest unit for my Christmas present. It played through the wireless.

On a visit to Orkney we had seen our first coloured slides at an illustrated talk in Kirkwall Town Hall by Lord Skene, who had served in the diplomatic service in the east, and recorded on slides his homeward journey through all sorts of exotic places, the names of which I regret I cannot recall after all this time. When we came out of the hall we remarked how we suddenly noticed the colour around us. Those slides had opened our eyes to fully appreciate our environment. We had to acquire a camera capable of such magic. I think our Kodak Bantam cost £12, a great deal for us at that time, but what hours of pleasure it gave to us and our visitors. If they found the showing of slides a boring, tedious ordeal to be endured, as nowadays many people, on occasions me included, profess to find it, they concealed such thoughts very successfully, and put on a tremendous act of enjoyment.

The Hislops were given to having Sunday evening sing-songs of Sankey hymns round the organ in their living room, and for through the week entertainment, taught us a card game called, I think, "Sevens".

Johnny was first to purchase a television set when electricity was installed at the station, so his hospitality always consisted of an invitation to view, followed by milky drinks.

Visiting lightkeepers sent to do temporary duty often provided interest and entertainment. There was Dugald from Islay, who brought his bagpipes and played them on summer evenings as he stood on the lighthouse balcony or as he marched along the cliff-tops beside the station. Pipe music with a background orchestration of sea and wind has a poignancy and appeal bagpipes never achieve anywhere else. Dugie tried to teach me how to fill in football coupons. "We will both do a bit," he'd say, "and then the luck of both of us will be on it." It never worked.

A hardworking pair of arrivals were lightkeeper Tom and his sister Katie. They set up camp with two tents on the hill above the station. Every spare minute they had they worked at their second occupation, which consisted of making the most beautiful jewellery, using thousands of

70

small cowrie shells known locally as "Groatie buckies". They cleaned each shell most carefully before stringing them, arranged by size, into necklaces. Matching earrings, brooches and pendants were also made. No varnish or colouring spoilt the pretty pale pinkish shells. Katie had the use of my iron while they were with us, and to say thank you presented me with a lovely necklace before she left. They had quite a successful little business, for the better craft shops in the Highlands all wanted to sell their products.

One temporary lightkeeper we had for a summer was a student at Edinburgh University doing a holiday job. He added to my interests in a more unusual way. He too liked to write, and throughout his stay wrote an article about the island, which eventually bought him a new suit. In his research for the article he came across the School Log, left mouldering away in the school, and shared his find with me before replacing it. It covered the period from 1870 to 1957, and in recording the day to day affairs of the school also chronicled the everyday life of the island.

The Honourable Society for Propagating Christian Knowledge "did settle one of their schools in the year 1723 with a salary of 200 merks to the teacher", who taught fifty, sixty or more of the children of the forty seven poor families who inhabited the island. I found out much later that the first school-master was George Gibson, whose wife was Katherine Rorieson of Thurso. She had been the sweetheart of John Gow, who became the notorious pirate of the north.

John, returning jubilant to Thurso with wedding dresses he had chosen for Katherine, discovered, on reaching port, that she had recently been married, in accordance with her father's wishes, to George Gibson. Even so, Katherine was prepared to leave all and go away with John. He departed furiously without her, but later, when she and her husband

71

had settled in Stroma, John Gow landed there hoping to take her away with him, or wreak revenge on George Gibson. We don't know what changed his mind, but he left without carrying out either of his intentions. The next we hear of him he's turned pirate, a career which landed him on the gallows.

In 1840 the teacher was paid £10, with £4 to his wife for teaching females to knit and sew. The subjects taught were English, reading, writing and arithmetic. "All between six and fifteen years of age can read, but the females are not commonly taught to write."

There were many unofficial holidays. On 8 August 1871, there was no school because both teacher and pupil teacher had to man a boat and fetch a midwife. There was no other able-bodied man on the island. They were all away fishing or piloting ships. The next day the services of the teacher alone were again called upon to ferry home the owner of the biggest farm, Mains of Stroma.

An inspector of 1874 remarks, "the Compulsory Clause is a dead letter in the island." When there were jobs to be done, or anything of unusual interest afoot, the children were simply not sent to school. When fish were plentiful the boys were kept home to catch them. In April the crops of oats and bere were sown, the gardens planted, the potatoes put in, and the children were employed in all these activities. Some of the bigger boys became herds for the summer and girls took posts in domestic service. Throughout May and June they cut and prepared their peats over on the Caithness mainland and took them home, and every pair of hands young and old were needed.

In May, the fathers departed to Shetland or to the west coast for herring fishing, and in August they departed to fish out of Wick. Some boys accompanied their fathers. The remaining children were expected to help with the sowing and hoeing of the turnips, the "cleaning" of the potatoes, and later to help gather in the harvest.

What with farm work, rough weather when they couldn't reach the school as they had no boots, and days off to visit that exciting caller the "Floating Shop", schooling was at times almost a sideline.

The church, too, instigated holidays. There was Thanksgiving for the harvest, and Fast days before Communion, which were known as Sacramental Holidays.

From other reading I found that, at one time, there were said to be two chapels on Stroma, Kirk of Stara and Kirk of Old Skoil. Then, in the seventeenth century, we find parishioners being "encouraged" to cross more frequently to worship in the church at Canisbay.

> *March 1654* — for moveing the people of Stroma to keepe ye kirk better, it is ordained yt no passenger comeing over to ye kirk sall pay any fraught. And if any yt hes boats stay away they shall pay 3sh 4d and others 40d.

> *About fifty years later* — . . . The presbytery enquired into Stromay, an Island in the Sea, belonging to the said parish (Canisbay) and found they were much neglected by reason of the Dangerous passage to that place, especially in winter, and whereas the Incumbent preached there twice a year and that in Summer only, the presbytery appointed him to preach there at least four tymes each year. . . ."

Where he preached I don't know for the church of our time was not built till 1878. A Baptist chapel was erected in 1877.

When we arrived on Stroma there were about eighty people living on the island. Theirs was the way of life of a crofting community. A few cows were kept, but the main form of livestock was sheep, and some folk kept a few hens as well. They grew vegetables — potatoes, cabbage and turnips — for their own use and small crops of oats and hay. We hadn't been there long when the population was down to fifty-five and the school roll to four. The main ways of earning a living were by lobster fishing and the manning of the post and supply boats.

Then the supply boat stopped. It was while Mr Hislop was Principal Keeper that the island's only shop closed down. He and Jimmy attended an island meeting during which the representative of the Scottish Wholesale Society, who owned the shop, offered to keep it open if the islanders were to reduce their charges for transporting the stock to the island. No agreement was reached. Old men recalled the burdens they used to carry on their backs, with no thought of remuneration, down the Huna shore to ship across to the island. The world had changed, and now those too old or frail to work boats on their own could obtain their necessities only by post, an expensive, impractical method.

The island's death knell was being sounded.

The Lighthouse Board arranged to finance a boat crossing for the station's provisions once a week. Mr and Mrs Hislop travelled to Wick to make arrangements with Lipton's the grocer, and a butcher.

Mr Hislop was a stocky, broad-built man with chubby, pink cheeks and dark eyes that very rarely viewed the world solemnly. He enjoyed telling and hearing anything humorous. Whenever he came in and I was baking he always enquired solicitously with a sniff, "Somethin' burnin'"? And I always fell for it, and checked the oven while he made off chuckling away to himself.

Mrs Hislop had a generous heart ready to spill loving kindness on everybody and every creature that came her way. I experienced her kindness often, especially when, after foolishly standing out talking to people in the fog, dressed only in a thin blouse and skirt, I caught a chill and was rather ill for some time. I turned completely yellow and felt nauseated the whole time. A locum came over

74

from Canisbay, who didn't seem able to diagnose what was wrong with me, nor to do anything about it. I hadn't yet turned yellow when he saw me. It was Bessie, the island nurse, who cleared up my nausea. She made me drink a stiff potion of bicarbonate of soda, which simply exploded inside and put an end to my sickness.

Mrs Hislop didn't come off so well when one morning she staggered back from the low east side beach. She'd fallen on the slippery rocks, knocked herself unconscious and, when eventually she'd come to herself, somehow managed to reach home. Mr Hislop called me in to see what could be done about her bleeding head. There was a huge lump on the back of her head. I parted the hair from it and agreed with her that we should just wrap a bandage round till she reached the doctor in Canisbay, across the very turbulent Sound of that day. When Dr Gill touched the lump, blood spurted from it with great force and profusion. Thank goodness I hadn't meddled. It was touch and go that the crossing was possible that day. Next morning she was out in the wash house coping with her laundry. Mrs Hislop was a plucky soul.

One day Mr and Mrs Hislop met a group on its way to destroy a dog that persisted in killing hens. She at once took pity on the unfortunate animal and begged to take him home. She loved that dog, and he returned that love wholeheartedly.

Imagine her sorrow when one day he disappeared, only to be returned from the other end of the island guilty, again, of hen slaughter. No further chance was granted by the incensed owner of the poultry, so Mr Hislop had to lead him away and have him shot.

She found solace in three other pets. On one outing to Orkney the Hislops arrived back with three companions — Josie, Nanny and Billy Goat. As that trio trip-trapped through the station gateway I thought, "Why, they look like devils", not a very original thought I suppose when one is faced by a combination of slanting eyes and sets of horns, but oh how true a description of that wicked Billy.

Mrs Hislop, as was only to be expected, loved all three, but on Billy especially did she lavish affection. He became more and more aggressive, and she wouldn't hear of tethering up the "poor lad".

Soon a walk became a nightmare for you never knew when that white brute would appear and attack.

Mr James Allan, our elderly Occasional Keeper, standing peacefully viewing the scene on the edge of the cliff turned round just in the nick of time to sidestep a charge from Billy that would have shot the old man over the cliff edge.

Jimmy, feeding our hens, fortunately heard the hooves thudding in his direction in time to jump into the henhouse and close the door. After the immediate, resounding biff on the door there followed a rather mysterious silence, and when Jimmy ventured to look out, there was the goat retreating in what seemed a rather crestfallen manner. As Jimmy reclosed the henhouse door he noticed a pale pink fragment adhering to its edge. It didn't take long to identify it as a bit of Billy's ear. I could feel no sorrow.

Chapter Seven

WHEN we first came to Stroma there were two ancient lorries and some tractors for island transport, and ordinary bicycles at the lighthouse.

As people continued to leave the island, vehicles became fewer and fewer. Jimmy purchased the one small, dilapidated lorry for the princely sum of £4, and when I took my first trip in it, and had to walk part of the way beside it, as Jimmy could not see through the discoloured windscreen, and the steering and brakes left much to be desired, I assured him he'd been robbed even at £4. Jimmy then arranged for his 500cc International Norton, complete with silver side-car, manufactured entirely by him for me, to be taken to Stroma by the lighthouse ship *Pole Star*. Soon the Norton was the only vehicle on the island. The rough roads played havoc with its tyres, where-upon Jimmy ruefully changed them with the wheels from his £4 lorry, and when we left Stroma we left the sorry spectacle behind.

Years later he had a letter from the editor of the magazine *Motorcycling*. He had traced the bike to Jimmy, and now wished to come and reclaim it with Bob Spreadbrow, a motor-cyclist who'd won the Clubman's Grand Prix on it at Brooklands in 1934. They hoped to write an article on their journey to get the Norton, and to refurbish it to look as it had at the time of its triumph.

Jimmy was sorry to have to tell of its demise, but Mr Spreadbrow and a friend called on us anyhow to show Jimmy photographs taken during and after the race.

By and by the lighthouse was equipped with a huge, gleaming blue Fordson Tractor and trailer, and this combination became the only vehicle on the island, and was pressed into service for all sorts of jobs, including funerals. I never attended one, but Jimmy sometimes drove "the hearse". In Stroma, as was the custom in many other places, the corpse, while in the house, lay in an open coffin amidst the mourners.

The island's cemetery was on the south east point. Its site had been chosen in the seventeenth century by a laird of the island, John Kennedy, who built the two-storied mausoleum which still dominated the place.

The islanders referred to him as "the owld Pirate", for the traditional story was that he had come to the island with two chests of gold each requiring twelve men to lift it, and plenty more impressive belongings. To the people there at that time, such riches could only have been acquired through piracy.

"Pirate" Kennedy then asked the islanders to build a house for him, promising to pay them well. They said he'd once captured a Greek merchantman, looted it and carried off the merchant's daughter to be his bride. This Grecian princess, as she was sometimes described, was said to have

78

knowledge of the medicinal properties of plants, and made a herb garden to supply herself with remedies.

We found out through a librarian friend, Mr Evan MacGillivray, who came to visit Mr and Mrs Hislop, that John Kennedy had originated from Kinmuck or Kermunckes (there are various forms of the name), an estate in Aberdeenshire.

We used to hunt for any trace of the Kennedy house. We were pretty sure we knew the area in which to look, for one day when Jimmy was visiting old Andy and Kate, our nearest neighbours on the north end, he picked up a valuable clue. Their horse had strayed, and in explaining its whereabouts to her husband the wife said, "It's down at Kermuckes". Jimmy asked where exactly Kermuckes was, and what was to be found there, whereupon they both vehemently denied all knowledge of any place of that name!

According to a writer around 1724 — "On the North side lyes the principall dwelling house built by Kennedy of Kairnmuck". When George Low visited the island in 1774, he saw in the Uppertown (at the north end), "the remains of a pretty large house and gardens once possessed by a gentleman, the proprietor of the island . . ."

Who, then, were the Kennedys and why did they go to live on the remote island of Stroma?

The Kennedy family were hereditary Constables of Aberdeen, an office which, according to some sources, came to the family about 1308, when a Kennedy led a force on behalf of Robert Bruce against Edward I's garrison in the Castle of Aberdeen. The castle was demolished, but nevertheless the hereditary title and dignity of the Constableship of Aberdeen was bestowed on Kennedy for the leading part he had played in the successful attack.

The Kennedys were then living on a piece of raised ground between Shiprow and the Green in Aberdeen, and had a private chapel there dedicated to St Katharine, the family's patron saint. The place, named after the chapel, was called St Katharine's Hill.

With the office of Constableship came "haill privilidges, liberties, proffeits, commodities belonging to the said office". When, in 1591, Kennedy of Carmuck, Constable of Aberdeen, died and was buried in St Nicholas Church, special permission, on payment of £10, was given by the Magistrates and Town Council for the mourners to wear black clothes and carry arms at the funeral. A Kennedy was a person of some standing in the community.

In 1431, Thomas Kennedy set about acquiring an estate for himself. He was already a landowner in the Ellon area, having as headquarters a stone tower known as Kinmuck. Now he bought more land in the vicinity, including the hill of Ardgith, the site of the present Ellon Castle. There, between 1413 and 1500, the family erected a "tour fortalice", of which the foundation and wall remains can still be seen in the ruin known as the Old Castle of Ellon, which lies alongside the driveway to the present house.

In 1629, the Kennedy family, by then established in the Ellon area for two centuries, nearly doubled the extent of their property by buying the Barony of Ardgrain and various other lands around their original holdings.

They were obviously prosperous and successful; in 1634 they presented a beautiful silver communion cup to the church in Ellon. The donors were John Kennedy and his wife Janet Forbes, and their choice of beaker denotes people of considerable taste and refinement.

A few years after this gift was made, came the time of the Covenant followed by the Civil War. John Kennedy and an old friend and neighbour, Thomas Forbes of Watertown, were on the Covenanting side, and together they hunted priests and attended meetings of the cause in Aberdeen and even as far away as Glasgow.

Their friendship was to come to a sudden and tragic end on the 13 February 1652, when Forbes of Watertown, at the head of an armed band of thirty-two men, sprang into action to put a stop to a project by the Kennedy family.

John Kennedy the Elder and his erstwhile soldier son, John the Younger, were approaching the public highway with a drainage ditch, which they intended to continue through the road. Watertown and his fellow objectors would not allow them to do this, despite a promise to bridge the cutting adequately and not cause inconvenience.

The Watertown force galloped down upon the six by the ditch, and discharged a volley of stones against them. One fell, but the others, men of courage and determination, advanced to close with their attackers, John the Elder wielding, to considerable effect, a great two-handed sword.

Suddenly, into their midst dashed the local minister, ordering hostilities to cease. In the lull of about seven minutes that followed, John Kennedy the Elder offered to withdraw if Watertown did likewise, but old Kermuckes had overlooked the spirit of his soldier son. A furious John the Younger, battered and bleeding, declared that he and his men would not "stir a foot", until the last Watertown man was within "their nether yett", and then, his hatred for his enemies white hot, he commanded the workmen to get on with digging the ditch.

That was that. Stones again bombarded the Kennedys. One struck John the Elder on the cheek, knocked out three of his teeth and broke his jaw. His revenge was immediate. In a fury of pain and anger he charged in among his assailants and cleft their leader's skull with a blow from his great sword. Thomas Forbes of Watertown fell to the ground, paralysed and mortally wounded. Four months later he was dead.

81

John Kennedy the Elder went to put his case to the authorities in Edinburgh, where, because of accusations made by the Forbes family, he was thrown into prison. Somehow he made his escape, and when, on 15 October, the Kennedy party was called to trial, none of the fighting men appeared. They were then declared rebels and outlaws.

For five more years John the Elder's wife continued to live at Ardgith, and the widow of Forbes of Watertown continually took out warrants for the arrest of the fugitives — John the Elder and John the Younger — whom she claimed were frequently seen in the area.

In 1657 the Kennedy family sold all their Aberdeenshire lands and, by 1659, the two Johns were asking for the removal of their excommunication from the church. As the Synod of Aberdeen recommended that the Caithness Presbytery grant their request, we may reasonably assume that the family had settled there.

In October of that same year, the older Kennedy was appointed an elder for Stroma in the church of Canisbay on the north coast of Caithness. This was the year he had obtained a wadset (mortgage) for Stroma from the Earl of Caithness. He was once more a laird, this time of an island two and a half miles long by one mile wide amidst the tempestuous tides of the Pentland Firth.

We know very little of how the family lived in their new situation. They appear to have taken an interest in the church and had a seat for themselves installed in the one at Canisbay. They also seem to have created gardens and to have taken a keen interest in botany and medicine. A writer around 1724 says: "As to Plants, Cairmuks a Gentleman there, who studies Medicine, can give the best account . . ."

They crossed the Firth to Orkney where, in Kirkwall, John Kennedy the Elder obtained a house called The

Gallery, on a charter from the Town Council. In *Kirkwall inthe Orkneys* it is stated that "In Kirkwall, Kennedy soon came to be a trusted public man".

In 1677, John Kennedy of Carmunck was appointed an arbiter in the division of an Orkney estate. This would have been the soldier son, for John of the Great Sword is thought to have died about 1672. That is the date on the Kennedy mausoleum in which, sadly to my mind, they continued to make a name for themselves after death.

They were not buried, their bodies being laid out in the vault, and owing to chemical properties in the air they were preserved, though not embalmed, and "were wont to be exhibited as curiosities". Macfarlane in his *Geographical Collections Relating to Scotland* written about 1724, says that the bodies placed there in coffins "forty years ago and upwards to this day have all the members intire, and so firmly dryed up that they will stand upright on their feet. . ." A traveller, Pococke, who toured Scotland in 1760 also remarks on the phenomenon, explaining the preservation as the result of "nitre in the air".

The Right Reverend Robert Forbes, who wrote journals of his *Episcopal Visitations* in 1762 and 1770, says he decided not to cross to Stroma because the bodies had been interred. However, he interviewed a man who forty years earlier had visited the house of Murdoch Kennedy, a descendant of John of the Great Sword. Murdoch showed little reverence for his family, and, as was his wont with visitors, took the man to the tomb where by "setting a Foot on one of his Father's, made the Body spring up and speedily and salute them". He then laid the body down again, and proceeded to "beat a march upon the Belly, which sounded equally loud with a Drum".

Another disgraceful scene was said by the Stroma folk to have taken place in this gruesome vault in 1721. This was when William Sinclair of Freswick visited the tomb, accompanied by two witnesses and equipped with a document on which there was traced the signature of the last Kennedy. William Sinclair placed a pen in the dead man's hand and guided it over the traced signature. His fellow conspirators witnessed the signature, and so the Laird of Freswick acquired the island.

Vandalism ends the sorry tale. When George Low visited Orkney and Shetland in 1774 he too went to Stroma in the hope of seeing the celebrated mummies. All he saw in the mausoleum were a couple of skulls and a collection of bare bones lying about amongst sheep dung. The islanders told him how some of the many people who had come to see the mummies had broken down the door and destroyed the bodies. The door had not been replaced, and sheep and cattle had got in and trampled to pieces what was left.

A septuagenarian friend of ours on Stroma told how the youths of his day played football with "the owld Pirate's" skull and chased the girls with his long leg bones.

How are the mighty fallen!

Chapter Eight

IT WAS agonising to see home after home stripped and left bare. Blank windows gaped at us like the unseeing eyes of stunned creatures. Some of the older people were very distressed about having to leave. Old Andy became withdrawn and wouldn't speak. James Allan said that he felt sure some day other people would come and settle on Stroma. William Bremner maintained that had the island been one of Orkney's numerous group it would have been better served than it had been as Caithness's solitary island.

The story of how Stroma came to belong to Caithness is rather strange. Unspecified venomous animals were said to have lived on the island. Some were taken to Orkney, some to Caithness. Those brought to Orkney died but those taken to Caithness survived, and so it was said Stroma came under the authority of Caithness. There were neither rats nor hares on Stroma when we were there, but what the venomous animals were I've no idea.

The school shut and Mrs Thomson, the teacher, was offered a post "on the other side", as the Stroma folk called the mainland of Caithness. We were delighted when Mr T decided to stay on alone in the schoolhouse for a year.

He still came down to us to listen to "Saturday Night Theatre" on the radio, or cut Jimmy's hair, or have his cut by Jimmy, or just to spend the evening in all sorts of discussion. If the haircutting and discussion coincided, Jimmy would experience quite a few painful moments, for Mr T, as he became engrossed in what was being said, would unwittingly press the comb down on the victim's scalp.

Sometimes we'd all take a turn outside to look at the sea, and perhaps watch a liner outlined in lights glide by in the darkness. As it rocked in the tides Mr T would say with a chuckle, "It's all right, ladies. We always experience a little motion here. This is the Pentland Firth."

It was an evening scene over the Firth that got me started at last on the first article I ever wrote.

After less than a year on the island I found myself in love with it, and felt inspired to write a sonnet about it. A friend of my father's had given him a year's subscription to the *Scots Magazine* and he passed each copy on to us. I sent my attempt at a sonnet praising Stroma to the editor. But Mr Daw wrote back tactfully to say that they did not often publish poetry, but he felt his readers would be interested in my life on the island if I were to write about it. Thrilled to bits, for I'd always had an ambition to be a writer, I tried and tried to get going on an article. I didn't tell anybody except Jimmy what I was doing, as I didn't think anybody would be interested, so when my article eventually appeared it was greeted with great surprise, and, I'm glad to say, approval by my fellow islanders. Mr T, however, at tea in our house with some talkative friends, cautioned them roguishly, "Watch what you're saying. There's a chiel amang ye takin' notes". How right he was!

Eventually, one night after a trip to the back gate, I had my beginning, and once started, the words flowed, and I began my first article — "My Home on Stroma":

Since I came into the house, about half an hour ago, I haven't been able to hear the lamp's gentle hiss or the crackles from the black stove. This is because I have been down at the sea, and my ears are still full of its sounds.

Twenty yards from our back gate lies the Pentland Firth. Tonight, it is like a great stage, alive with a thousand silken skirts, swaying and swishing to an eternal accompaniment of throbbing wind. Along the shore's edge, white froth ruffles and curtseys like layers of lacy petticoats. I have "gazed and gazed", as I have done so many times in the few months I have lived here, on the most northerly tip of the island of Stroma, and I hope, like the poet, the procession of beautiful pictures I have enjoyed will, all my life, "flash upon that inward eye".

And they have — often by conscious recall — sometimes in dreams.

There was a bite in the coastline to the west of the light-house where the flat rocky shelves reminded me of a Roman amphitheatre, and I dubbed it "the theatre". There, when Jimmy was on duty, I'd sit alone listening to that lovely sound of ripples plucking tinkling music from pebbles. Stately liners, cargo ships of all kinds and countries, and seine net fishing boats cut smooth courses through a blue, ribbon-like length of summer sea. Nearer the shore, the Stroma men, who had an inherited knowledge of the powerful tides and touchy temper of the waters round their island, fished for lobsters. It was fascinating to watch them, as they kept the little boats out of the tide's grip, circling continuously while they worked at their creels. Bobbing families of eider ducks, like the

87

colourful contents of a rag bag emptied on the satin sea, cooed softly as they glided past. Rolling grey seals popped up inquisitive, whiskered faces to gaze at me with large liquid eyes. Cinnamon-headed, sapphire-eyed gannets plummeted into the water like kamikaze pilots. White foam trailed across brown rocks making lacy bridal trains.

If it wouldn't be such a trek and nuisance to my family I think I'd like to be buried beside "the theatre" in Stroma.

I remember one day after I'd been sitting there in the afternoon seeing, as I walked home, that Jimmy was dangling halfway down the tower on the lime-washing stage. Lime-washing time was the only blot on the summer days.

As soon as we got a settled spell of good weather the dreaded lime-washing of the whole station took place. While we were on Stroma, a Principal Keeper further south had been lime-washing a tower on behalf of an unfit colleague at another station, and had fallen to his death when the lime-washing stage became unhooked and hurtled to earth with him on it. After that, regulations about the stage attachments were tightened and all hooks had to be replaced with screwed shackles.

Even so, the oiling of the tower's copper dome was still done by the men moving freely and unharnessed over it, using the footholds and handholds spaced here and there on the dome. Jimmy only let me know when that job was over.

I was always relieved too when the stage was put past for the year. At that time, before the fatal accident I mentioned, it consisted of a wooden platform fixed to a series of ropes by hooks, the openings of which had to be "mouseled", that is closed over by string. The ropes were attached to the balcony rail that encircled the light room, and each keeper in turn was lowered bit by bit down the tower, lime-washing as he progressed.

The nice side to the lime-washing was the picnics. The men were so bespattered with lime that they had to get out of their working clothes before entering the houses, and to save them the effort of changing so often the wives in turn provided picnics for a coffee break in the morning and for tea in the afternoon.

We all gathered together on the grassy edge between the wall and the cliff edge, and enjoyed a pleasant social occasion in the sun. Oh, happy times on Stroma! I remember my beloved grandmother so enjoying those events, and Mr T used to join us too. We were a happy band of people by the summer sea, over which long lines of guillemots flittered by, strung out like necklaces of black and white beads, and fulmar petrels glided and swooped glided and swooped, with effortless grace.

But our happy times with the Hislops were soon to end, for among the people steadily streaming away from the island, now that the school and shop had closed, was Bessie the nurse, who was also the wife of an islander. Mr Hislop had to have regular medical treatment, and with Bessie's departure this was no longer possible, so he had to be posted.

Sadly we said goodbye to Mr and Mrs Hislop.

Our next Principal Keeper and his wife were Mr and Mrs Robert Thomson. Jimmy, though heir apparent to the goats, because he was the one who milked the nannies when Mrs Hislop wasn't there, declined to accept them, and they were left to the Thomsons.

We happily went over to "Millac", a powdered milk which suited us fine.

Soon old grey Nanny produced a black and white kid, which the Thomsons named Sheila and adopted into their household, which already consisted of a small dark-coloured Shetland collie and a pure white budgerigar.

When Mr and Mrs Thomson went on leave, the budgie

was lodged with us and the dog with Johnny, the Second Assistant.

During the budgie's first stay we called it Joey, but it revealed our ignorance to its owners. "Have you been callin' the budgie Joey?" demanded Mr Thomson. "His name is Buddy." Buddy had told on us.

I've never before or since seen a budgie who could talk so much and so clearly. Indeed, I used to say to Jimmy we could never get away from the Thomsons, for when they went off the island there was Buddy in our living room, first speaking in Mrs Thomson's Border accents and then in Mr Thomson's Shetland voice.

Buddy was allowed out of his cage only when I was out of the room, for as with my terror of hens, I couldn't bear a feathered creature fluttering near me in an enclosed space. One night Jimmy became quite alarmed. Buddy was out having his time of freedom, and, as was his custom, alighted on Jimmy's finger. Jimmy thought he should know his surname as well as his Christian name and said to him a few times, "Buddy Thomson, Buddy Thomson". Buddy listened and then hunched himself up, fluffed up his feathers and strained as though making a tremendous effort. Jimmy feared the bird was going to have a heart attack or something. Then out it came as clear as a bell, "Buddy Thomson. Buddy Thomson". He was a quick pupil.

Sheila Goat-Thomson was not a slow learner either. The Thomsons included her on outings as well as taking her into the house for visits. But soon she noticed if Jimmy and I were leaving the station, and made up her determined mind that she was coming too. She trotted along quite contentedly, but if we stopped to look through the binoculars she disapproved and reminded us with a none too gentle butt that we were out walking with her. I took to placing a walking stick between her and me. Jimmy always lifted me over fences. Now Sheila stopped at each one and bleated and bleated, demanding to be lifted over too.

The Thomsons, however, were not long with us. Again health problems and no medical aid on the island made a posting necessary.

By this time there was only one island family of four left. Fortunately they took over the goats, and kept them enclosed, which was a great relief to me.

About this time a young couple, John and Cathie Lade, replaced Johnny, the Second Assistant. After quite a short stay Cathie left the island to be under medical care while she had her lovely baby girl, Catherine. We welcomed their return, and all adored the baby.

Our new Principal Keeper and his wife arrived, Mr and Mrs Robert Crowe, a handsome, charming couple whose company we thoroughly enjoyed. They became our Canasta partners. I think somebody must have given us that card game as a present. We found it a fascinating and engrossing game to play, with its forming of "melds" and "canastas", great excitement, great fun! One evening my deep involvement in the game nearly ended in catastrophe.

Jimmy had been over in Wick having a tooth extracted. I told our Supernumerary — a Canasta addict — that I'd get everything comfortable and in order for Jimmy's return, and light the fire in our sitting or "best" room so that Jimmy could relax comfortably there for the evening.

Jimmy did not feel too bad after his ordeal, and decided he was fit for a game of Canasta in the evening with Jim and me.

Eventually, I went through to the kitchen to prepare a supper tray. Before carrying it through I set two kettles of water on the paraffin cooker to heat for filling our hot water bottles.

Back I went to the sitting room. We had supper. Then the game started afresh, and all other thoughts went out of my head.

The evening drew to a close. I piled the supper things back on the tray, and returned to the kitchen/living room. Well, I couldn't believe my eyes, nor think what had happened. The room was festooned with long, black sooty threads. They dangled everywhere and a choking, sooty, oily smell pervaded the room.

After the minute or two it took for me to take in the scene, I rushed through for Jimmy and Jim. They stared aghast for a minute. Then Jimmy, ever reasonable and practical, said "The Valor has flared". We turned to the paraffin stove — black smoke belched out of it and the kettles were furred black. "They're not safe to leave", warned Jimmy.

Then both men insisted I go to bed and they would deal with the sorry state of affairs. When I got up next morning it was to find a sparkling, thoroughly spring-cleaned room. They'd worked till 3 am! Little did I deserve such consideration. After all I'd been the culprit.

Chapter Nine

THOUGH we never found the Kennedys' house, there were extant on the island other houses with interesting snippets told about them. One was "The White House".

It was whitewashed and two storeys high. It stood by the north end pier, and had been left almost totally furnished. Its furniture was rather unusual. There were mirrors and stands entwined with griffins, heavily carved sideboards and tables and glass-fronted, velvet-lined cabinets.

It had been deserted before we came to the island, but not for the usual reasons.

The story was that it had been occupied by incomers, a family of four — husband, wife, son and daughter. Wife had been a nurse and she and daughter made it their business to call upon the aged and infirm. Sad to say the aged and infirm discovered that they were less well off financially after such visits.

At last, one old lady checking her savings after the visitors left, found that several pounds had been removed. However, she had the numbers of the notes, and went to the Post Office to report her loss. The Postmaster immediately contacted the police in Wick, where mother and daughter had gone for an outing. The police followed them round the town picking up the stolen notes as they spent them. They were arrested. Whereupon the remainder of the family immediately made themselves scarce.

A morse signalling lamp accompanied by a coded message found in one of the rooms told another story, whether one of loneliness or simply romance in action, I don't know. The message gave the girl's name and address and said words to the effect "I will write to you if you write to me". I wonder if any lonely sailor took up the suggestion.

After we had settled on Stroma, the Thomsons at the Schoolhouse received a letter from the former occupants of the White House asking them to sell their belongings for them.

Mr and Mrs T organised a sale. Some of the people who'd had money stolen objected passionately to this. They, not unnaturally, felt that in the first place they should be recompensed.

However, the sale went ahead and quite a few people came. Jimmy bought me "Marie", a Royal Doulton figure, and three small ivory elephants.

There was a cottage where an old woman had lived who augmented her income by selling fair winds to sailors. I often wondered just exactly what happened in such transactions. I found out how it was carried out on one occasion when I came across a poem by David Grant, who was schoolmaster in Canisbay from 1857 to 1861. The poem is called "The Witch's Wind". Four men from Mey on the north coast of Caithness crossed the Pentland Firth in their yawl to Longhope on the island of Hoy in Orkney to buy cattle. While doing their business the winds, which had been fair for their crossing, veered west-nor'-west and strengthened to gale force. For four long, impatient days they were storm-bound in Longhope. An Orkney man jocularly suggested they "trade for a wind" with an old bearded woman called Canny Jess. The skipper, who claimed he'd all his life called winds to his aid by whistling for them, refused to have anything to do with the old woman, but the other three without telling him, slipped along to her cottage with a quarter of tea to use for trading with Jess.

Jess first insisted that the tea be brewed and tasted to see if it was good, and then she ordered one of them to go to their boat and fetch a bucket. This done, she took the bucket into another room and the fisherman puffed their pipes uneasily and wished they hadn't come, as animal noises such as clucking, caterwauling and grunting issued from the ben end.

An hour later the old woman reappeared with the bucket in which there were now three small wisps of straw each tied with a bit of wool.

She then instructed them to place the bucket as near the prow as possible, and forecast where on two occasions the wind would drop on their journey. When this happened, one of the bundles had to be cast into the sea each time, but the third one had to be kept till they were safely home in Mey.

They set off, and sure enough it was as Jess had said, and on carrying out her instructions, favourable winds blew up at once.

A cable-length from their home haven, the skipper, scornful of the whole performance, pitched the last bundle into the sea. Immediately all went dark, thunder bellowed

95

and the sea rose in anger and threatened to swamp the boat. They didn't know in what direction they were going. Their only concern was to keep afloat and alive.

When at last the storm abated, they looked around them. They were back at Longhope, almost at the witch's door.

"Ah, well!" quoth Will, "you may call it a yarn,
But I tell you it's Gospel true."

Down at the south west corner a house was pointed out to us where the man had been so poor he had done his ploughing by yoking his ox and his wife to the plough.

Nearby were the remains of a building on a rock stack, sixty to seventy feet off shore. This stack was called Castle of Nestag, and the islanders thought that it had been the situation of a Norse fortress and had been connected to the island by a drawbridge. Mr T was of the opinion it had been a stronghold of the last great viking, Sweyn Asleifson.

We know from the Orkneyinga Saga that Sweyn did come to Stroma, but there is no mention of his having a residence there. Indeed from the story he had little choice over where to lay his head for the night.

In 1155 at the time of Lent, Sweyn was being chased by Earl Harold. When the earl saw Sweyn's boat at the Stroma shore he "suspected that the mens' homes must be fairly near". This would suggest that men from Stroma joined "that ultimate Viking" in his harryings and carousels.

A gale of wind arose, and neither Sweyn nor Harold could get off the island. A diplomatic resident called Amundi persuaded the adversaries to keep to terms of peace previously agreed upon for the winter, and then to clinch the deal "got both of them into one bed, Earl Harold and Sweyn".

Another mouldering ruin was The Mains of Stroma.

96

This had been the biggest farm on the island, and consisted of a farmhouse and steading, known as The Mains of Stroma, and a house where the family who owned the farm had lived, which was known as The Cottage. The apparent ravages to these buildings were said to be due to the assiduous attentions of woodworm.

The Cottage was still roofed and consisted of many rooms in which were many built-in beds, commonly, but erroneously, known (so Jimmy tells me) as box-beds. A real box bed is not built into the wall but stands independently on the floor all "boxed" in.

Jimmy discovered a trap door in the floor of the cottage which opened on to a place of concealment which he immediately suspected, rightly or wrongly, as having been a hideaway for smuggled goods.

Smuggling had been indulged in in the past. Our septuagenarian friend, Mr William Bremner, told us how one night he, then a small boy, had heard his father leave the house. He got out of bed and followed unnoticed, until it was too far and late for his father to return him home.

They came to the harbour where several people were already launching boats to sail out to a Dutchman lying off the island. William and his father joined the flotilla, and soon the boy found himself on board the ship.

William recalled the crew as the "prettiest" men — in shirts of red and blue and striped trousers with brightly coloured patches. All round the ship were shelves of gleaming bottles of brandy and perfume and reddish brown wooden boxes of tobacco. William's prize that night was a small, glass-stoppered bottle of Eau de Cologne which he reluctantly shared out in precious drops on ladies' Sunday handkerchiefs.

Such adventures could end in disaster.

In 1825 there was only one room vacant in the inn at Huna when a military gentleman and his new wife arrived. They were horrified to discover they were to have company in their bedroom. Six smugglers from Stroma, rowdily drowning their sorrows, for they'd been caught red-handed and had had to relinquish their haul to the excise officer, suggested bawdily that the bridegroom take one of the three box beds, while they shared the remaining two.

There were certainly plenty of willing buyers for the duty-free goods, but there were also plenty of excise men out to confiscate the cargoes.

One old lady with a strong belt, honeycombed with pockets round her waist, chatted to an excise officer, while her skirts bulged over a sixty pound wad of tobacco. As he stamped to and fro beside her, he was treading on neat turf patches fitted over cavities filled with smuggled goods. Later this gentleman claimed to have *stamped* out smuggling in the north — a remark which amused many people.

A little cave called The Malt Barn, in the Big Gloup, a gigantic blowhole in the island's surface, was the hiding place for the whisky still. The "Big Gloup" was an abyss 150 yards from the cliff edge and was more than 100 feet deep, 100 yards long and about 80 yards wide. Except for one steep, grass-covered slope, its sides were walls of rock reverberating to the hushing and roaring of the waves, as they washed in through the straight narrow channel that stretched to the sea, and swilled round the bottom of the cavern in a creamy froth. The Malt Barn, only accessible at ebb tide, was a safe hiding place for the still.

There was a "Little Gloup" too which took the form of a gash about 20 yards long and only a few feet wide. I used to be quite alarmed sometimes at the suddenness with which we found ourselves on the brink of those treacherous holes. It was possible to enter the smaller gloup at ebb tide through a dark tunnel starting from the shore. Jimmy did this. I wasn't brave enough, and was very relieved when his voice told me he was coming towards daylight again.

About 1830 some Stroma men were caught selling illicit spirits to shop-keepers and various people in Orkney. On their way to trial in Kirkwall, a gale caught them, and off the South Ronaldsay coast they were swamped in the strong tide race, and all were lost.

Not long after this incident, the whisky still was thrown over the cliffs into the sea. Better times had come, and when it was possible to earn a living without the more risky side-lines, they were given up.

The white and herring fishing took an upward turn, and Stroma fishermen sailed further afield in their "firthies" and "zulus", catching fish in such quantities near Barra and around Shetland that Stroma became the second fishing port of Caithness. The fish were dried and salted and sent to Billingsgate and even as far as Spain.

Farming methods were improved. The spade and sickle that had laboriously coped with cultivation of land laid out in wasteful strips were now replaced by plough and scythe that could deal with economically viable areas.

Chapter Ten

MORNING, noon and night, our man on duty switched on the Marconi radio telephone in the wireless room, and waited till a lightkeeper in Stromness, Orkney, said "Stromness calling Stroma, are you receiving me Stroma? Over", and from our side went out "Stroma replying. Have you anything for us?" Then would probably follow comments on welfare and weather. On occasion a personal snippet would be passed to Jimmy's family in Deerness who always tuned in on their wireless. So we did hear voices from elsewhere every day, but often the only human beings we saw, apart from the folk at the lighthouse, were men passing on ships. A friendly wave was always exchanged if they were near enough to shore to see us. If they were further out one of the light-keepers would salute them by hoisting our flag and dipping it in greeting. Usually they replied.

One day we recognised one of Her Majesty's smaller

Royal Navy ships as being the one on which my brother-in-law served as boatswain. Jimmy raised the flag; they replied, and we waved and waved — I with tears flowing — to a small figure on the deck hectically waving his white-topped cap. Later we heard from Raymond that the captain, who knew something of the circumstances, had announced to the company over the relay system, "We are now approaching the lighthouse that belongs to the Buffer's brother-in-law". We'd come up in the world.

Another occasion, more closely associated with royalty, was when a passing fishing boat bore the Queen Mother away from the island. We'd been told in strictest confidence by a family friend that she was coming to Stroma to picnic and hoped to visit the lighthouse. Greatly excited, we cleaned and polished more diligently than ever. Jimmy, who was in charge at the time, ensured that the station was up to scratch, revealing to the others only that an important visitor was coming. I dealt with the house, for we even dared to hope the royal visitor might step inside. The day came and we waited and waited. A minister and his family arrived at the station bubbling over with how their visit had coincided with that of the Queen Mother and how they'd met her twice on the island. But now she had departed. We expected that the boat would land the distinguished passenger at the north end pier, since it wasn't far from the lighthouse, but very soon Johnny, the Second Assistant, arrived to say that a fishing boat had just passed with a lady seated in a chair on its deck, who'd waved to him. Imagine our disappointment! The sea had been too rough to come in to the north end pier.

Ships with which we were more involved were the annual coal boat and the Lighthouse ships, the *Pole Star* and *The Pharos*.

When the island was populated, the coming of the coalboat was quite an event. The evening she was due to arrive the islanders congregated at the pier to watch critically as one of their number piloted her in to her berth. The following day when the cargo was discharged it was all hands to work steadily from morn to night, with one short break to eat.

Some Stroma men filled buckets in the hold. The mate and engineer manipulated the winch. One man seated on the pier hauled the derrick over the pier while another on the ship hauled it back again to hover over the hole. A little black mountain of coal rose on the pier.

Some people weighed out the coal on weighing machines. Other workers filled up the sacks, a set of which each household provided for itself.

Other islanders arrived with horses and carts to transport the fuel to each house. Some of the folk from the distant north end took their share home by boat.

The first reference to an annual supply of coal for the island that I was able to find, was an entry in the School Log in July 1928, when the coal boat's coming caused the absence of a few of the senior boys.

In 1886 the School Board agreed to supply coals for the school fire, and in 1910, on May 8 and 10 — "The School was not opened as the Head had to attend to bringing coal to the Schoolhouse".

After this date, the frequent references throughout the School Log to "peat work" cease.

May saw the beginning of the "peat trade" as one teacher called it. The Stroma folk had to cross to the mainland of Caithness to cut their peats. They were cut, set up to dry, boated to the island, unloaded, carted home and built into stacks. This went on throughout May and June. In 1871 the teacher writes a little bitterly:

> *June 12* — "At this season of the year every child (almost) that is able to work is required — so I am informed."

102

June 30 — "Attendance small — only 36 present. Peats in some senses are a great nuisance."

Did he relent on July 10? — "More peats for the Teacher today."

Every year the *Pole Star* called with "the stores", the year's supplies for the station. It was like Christmas. Each household was presented with its share of goods — long bars of yellow washing soap, net cloths, zinc pails, pots and pans, tea-towels, replacements of bedding and furniture, and a smart new uniform for each keeper.

The ship's launches brought the cargo to the north end pier and sometimes also brought Jimmy Thomson, one of the ship's crew who belonged to the same Orkney parish as Jimmy and who tried always to pay us a call when the ship came to Stroma.

On one occasion as the keepers were winching the barrels of paraffin from the launch on to the pier, a freak wave rushed in and tossed the launch on to the pier, from which it tumbled back into the sea scraping its side. In a trice the boatswain had collected the escaped barrels bobbing about on the water and headed out to sea, till the danger had passed. I once heard a crew member on a tramp steamer refer scornfully to the men on the light-house ships as "rock hoppers", but I'm certain he was never in the dangerous waters with which they had to contend when working in treacherous conditions round the rocks and islands off our coasts.

Not every year, but thrice during our stay on Stroma, the lighthouse flagship, *The Pharos*, lay off the pier and sent in her launches. The Commissioners of Northern Lights were on their annual cruise round a certain number of lighthouses — said to be their only recompense for being members of the board. They were the sheriffs of Scotland's sea-board counties, and when introducing themselves said,

103

"I'm Ayr", or "I'm Fife".

In the distant past there was seemingly a great deal of "bulling up" done on word of the flagship's approach. Stoves were cleaned and no food cooked for fear of tarnishing them. The story went that the Secretary of the Board had on occasion been known to draw a handkerchief along the tops of doors to check if they had been dusted. Well, maybe! I must say I never saw anything of the kind happen.

Down the road they would come — a motley crew of mostly elderly gentlemen — some bowling merrily on, others tottering along on sticks. Irreverently my thoughts turned to Christina Rossetti's *Goblin Market*.

> *"Come buy", call the goblins*
> *Hobbling down the glen –*
> *One tramped at a rat's pace,*
> *One crawled like a snail,*
> *One like a wombat prowled, obtuse and furry,*
> *One like a ratel tumbled hurry-skurry.*

Then — once before breakfast — the whole party would invade one's house, to be precise *their* house, and we'd all sit trying to converse — they in their "plummy" public school voices, attempting to make light, amusing conversation.

Most of them tried to be pleasant. There was, of course, the odd one who did not. Once I explained how I had not been present on their previous visit because I had been ill.

"This is a perfectly, healthy place", snapped one aged person. He was going to nip any complaints in the bud.

As had been the way down the centuries, not all ships passed Stroma without mishap.

One evening John Manson, the younger son of the only remaining island family, arrived to tell us he'd heard on the short-wave radio that an Icelandic ship, *Dranga Yokul*, had just sunk off the lighthouse. The people had taken to a

104

life-raft and an oncoming trawler had rescued them all, including the skipper's wife and child. We rushed outside our wall, but apart from the receding trawler, not a sign of the episode was to be seen. The *Dranga Yokul* had sunk without trace.

As dawn broke on 3 February 1956, Jimmy made out a shape on the smaller of the Pentland Skerries, the two neighbouring islands to the south-east. He tuned in to the short wave radio and heard the Longhope and Wick life-boats discussing how best to take the crew off a 10,000 ton Norwegian tanker grounded on the smaller Skerry. Soon we were able to make her out as she lay helpless, the seas breaking over her.

The Longhope lifeboat thought the only chance was to land on the Skerry, and take the men off by breeches-buoy. They tried, but it was impossible to get into the Skerry. I listened in a turmoil of anxiety. It was terrible to think of those men in danger nearby, and nobody finding it possible to save them.

Then two helicopters arrived on the scene, and with great wonder and relief we watched them winch aboard the shipwrecked mariners and fly over to John o' Groat's with them. By this time the frigate *Wizard* was steaming to and fro in the vicinity, and we heard on the news that her admiral had taken command of the rescue operation.

I rather think this was one of the earliest rescue operations by helicopter.

The *Daily Express* of Friday, 10 February carried the following advertisement.

<⊃⊃ The Lift behind the Lift ⊂⊂>
41 lives saved from grounded tanker

Last Friday, in the biggest helicopter sea-rescue on record, 41 lives were saved from the Norwegian tanker Dovrefjell on the rocks of the Pentland Skerries, Orkney, when two life-boats

The day following the shipwreck, a helicopter again appeared over the ship. From the news we discovered this was to land the captain and first officer, to check the condition of the ship.

In the afternoon Stroma boatmen took a Lloyd's agent out to the tanker. When they reached her, a steel lifeboat, which had jammed in the lowering, was hanging over the side of the ship and above their heads. They refused to approach till it was released, as they thought it dangerous in its present position. It was cut loose, and they brought it back to the island's haven.

Mr Allan, the older of our Occasional Keepers, took the younger's watches, as the captain of the *Dovrefjell* wanted as many men as possible from the island to come out and get hawsers ready for the tugs he was now expecting.

The crew's belongings were now removed from the vessel, and Johnny, our Second Assistant, looking through the telescope at the Post Office, reported seeing Italian motor bikes being landed at John o' Groat's. You would have thought the excitement over the tanker, which had been converted for cargo, was drawing to a close. But no, on Saturday the 11th the news buzzing over the island was that the Chief Constables from Wick and Kirkwall, and the police constable who'd been appointed to Mey ever

106

since the Queen Mother had bought her castle there, were coming to Stroma to enquire about things that had disappeared from the ship on the Skerries.

It wasn't until 29 March, however, that a squad of plain clothes policemen arrived on the island, equipped with "walkie talkies" and mine detectors. They searched the empty houses, and Jimmy saw a motor boat loaded with rubber dinghies pass on the way to search the caves.

When Joe, our younger Occasional Keeper, came to go on watch at midnight he said all they'd found was a tin of olive oil under a stone on the west side. Stroma was exonerated.

By this time the ship was far away. On 28 February we watched the tugs trying to re-float her, and they succeeded in doing so by noon of that day.

Stroma's life-saving brigade had shown their skill and saved lives on several occasions in the past when vessels had come to grief on the island itself. In our time it was of course very much undermanned, consisting only of the three remaining male islanders, Andrew Manson, senior, and his two sons Andrew and John, and the lightkeepers.

Nevertheless, they held practices, when they fired the rocket and set up the breeches-buoy. The lightkeepers asked what was expected of them if there was a wreck and they were on watch. They were told that their first duty was to keep the light revolving, that achieved, they should of course do what they could to save life.

One beautiful summer's day, when their practice was to be performed in the presence of the Area officer, this gentleman asked, "Now what would you do if a ship was lying wrecked out there?"

Andrew Manson, senior, with a twinkle in his eye, replied, "If there was a wreck out there today, I for one, would not be here". No doubt he was referring to the days when wrecks were hoped for, because they meant a windfall to the very poor people of the islands. A minister on the island of Sanday in Orkney, prayed that if there were to be wrecks, let them be on Sanday. It was said that at the building of the lighthouse on Stroma, the sound of a ship approaching the rocks reached the ears of the workmen, who promptly stopped tapping with their hammers, so that they gave no warning to prevent her striking the island.

Of course there were quite legitimate wrecks. Our septuagenarian friend, William Bremner, told us how on 27 July 1888, the steamer *Copeland* of Leith came ashore on a reef called Langatoun during dense fog. On board was a cargo of Icelandic ponies and the writer, Rider Haggard, returning from Iceland, where he had been collecting material for a book.

I don't know how they all got ashore, or how the story ended, but the schoolboys were delighted that they had to get off school to herd the ponies.

On 4 May of the same year the school log recorded, "Some children have been employed carrying wood which the people are now discharging from the ship ashore on the east side of the island".

Wrecks were so numerous that in 1894 it was decided that the "peerie light", a lantern set on a pole between the two most dangerous points, Swelkie and Langatoun, was inadequate, and Stroma Lighthouse was built. The peerie light's oil store, a small, brick building, still stood when we were there.

Even so on 12 June 1903 — "some of the children have been kept from school to go with food to their fathers who are engaged discharging the cargo of the *SS Corinthia* which stranded near the north end of the Island Last Sunday".

At a much later date, the *Pennsylvania* went onto the neighbouring island of Swona in thick fog. Stroma men, passing on their way to Orkney, reached her before the lifeboat. She was loaded with cars. When they were salvaged and shipped across to the mainland by Stroma boats, one islander, Will Simpson, travelled aboard a car in order to be able to say that he was the first person to cross the Pentland Firth by car.

Considering the Firth's record of disasters, it was little wonder that the Stroma men were frequently called upon to act as pilots. Competition to get these jobs was keen, and Stroma boats would go forty miles or more along the coast, and wait for days for the arrival of a ship from Calcutta with a cargo of jute or an East Indiaman homeward bound.

There was once a captain who was glad of no less than thirteen Stroma men. One summer morning about three o'clock, men preparing to go to their creels, saw a full-rigged ship, the *Lady Ruthven* of Greenock, drifting helplessly towards the beacon at the south-west corner of the island. In their eagerness to bag pilot's post and welcome fee, many of the volunteers arrived barefoot and wearing no jackets, at the *Lady Ruthven*. The captain welcomed them. He had been saddled with a scratch crew of land-lubbers, who had proved useless, and he asked thirteen Stroma men to come as crew as far as Greenock. They agreed to do this and, apart from dodging, sails reefed down to lower topsails, in a gale off Cape Wrath, they made an uneventful journey to Greenock. The captain did try to persuade them to continue to his initial goal, Cardiff, but they stuck to the bargain, and had a few grand days in Greenock entertained by a Stroma man who had settled there some time before.

These pilots were more fortunate than many of their profession. Frequently, the ship they had taken through the dangerous Firth could not touch land in this country to let them off. One pilot landed in Quebec in his slippers.

When such unpremeditated outings came to a happy conclusion, and they were able to find a ship that took them home, they were thereafter known by the name of the port to which they'd been carried — Jamaica, Savannah and so on.

At the time of the Press Gang and during the Napoleonic Wars, there was always the danger of a volunteering pilot finding himself made prisoner on the craft he'd come to aid.

Chapter Eleven

THE installation of electricity was a great event for us, hurtling our domestic arrangements pell-mell into the twentieth century.

The radio beacon had been switched on only when visibility was poor. From it ships and aircraft took their bearings. Then it was decided that the beacon should be on all the time, which meant the bank of lead acid accumulators that powered it had to be replaced by a more powerful source of electricity. Consequently, three new Ruston Hornsby generating engines were installed in the engine room.

Mr Ewan, a radio engineer, and Charlie and Angus, "two artificers", came to install them. We kept the two artificers. They were on the whole good company. In vain did Charlie try to teach me how to turn corners in a modern waltz. He spent much of his leisure time learning *Tam o' Shanter* and *The Cremation of Sam McGee* off by heart. He also slimmed with determination and very noticeable results, and I was not altogether pleased about the new shape with which he left, for I feared some of his acquaintances might think I'd starved him.

One night during the artificers stay, when Jimmy was in the lightroom on watch, he had an experience that set his pulses racing. He'd lit up, a process I always enjoyed watching. A brass container with two wicks was filled with methylated spirits, and lit. This was slid into position under the vapouriser. A brass cap was then removed from the top of the lamp, and replaced with a mantle resembling a huge gas mantle. The blinds around the lantern were then pulled up. Through the day they were kept drawn to prevent the sun from striking the lens and starting a fire. Next, Jimmy went down into the lightroom, where he opened the valves on paraffin and air containers. This done, the lens was set off on its revolutions. He then returned to the lamp by stepping through a gap in the moving lens. Finally, he held a lit wax taper above the mantle, and opened a valve to let the vapourised paraffin gas into the mantle, where it ignited. The light was "in".

He'd done all that, this particular night, and then gone out on the balcony to check on the visibility and count the other lights he could see. To the south-east Duncansby Head; to the east the Pentland Skerries; to the west Dunnet Head; in the north-west Cantick Head on the Orkney Island of Hoy and two permanently lit beacons, Torness and the Lowther. Each one seen had to be marked off in a book along with a note about the wind force and weather conditions. I used to love to go up the tower at lighting-up time and watch as each of our neighbours lights was lit. You felt you were one of a band of brothers.

112

and proud to be serving, in the words of the motto of the Northern Lighthouse service, "for the safety of all" — "In Salutem Omnium".

Anyhow, to carry out these duties Jimmy went out on the balcony and walked right round the tower before re-entering and closing the heavy door. Then there came a knock on that door over fifty feet from earth. A deep breath was taken and courage summoned before the door was opened — to reveal Charlie. He had gone up to the light-room, which he had found empty, stepped out through the open door, and unknowingly followed Jimmy round the balcony, arriving too late to re-enter, for the door was shut.

The artificers, helped by the lightkeepers, had no easy task, for holes had to be drilled through thick, strong, stone walls. This they did with a Warsop drill, which on at least one occasion, after a lengthy period of use, emitted carbon monoxide fumes that made them all ill. Charlie and Jimmy immediately retired to bed, but Angus slept off the effects in a chair in the living room, giving me a rather peculiar sensation, as he slept with one eye open.

My word, how hard they worked!

At last the three engines were installed and an electrician of a very relaxed nature, Willie, set about wiring up the three houses. So eager was he to bring about the magic moment of "switch-on" that he festooned the entire block with wires, which clashed in the wind and encircled the buildings with a garland of fire. A more senior gentleman had the entire job undone. However, at last we were successfully electrified.

There wasn't enough electricity produced for us all to have electric cookers, so calor gas stoves were provided However, each house was given a refrigerator and an electric heater, and we had enough power for a television set and clothes iron.

113

Our black and white television set was bought, out of order, in an auction by Jimmy's father for 25/-. He replaced a couple of valves, and sent it, now working perfectly, to us.

The one programme we watched in those early days that has stuck in my mind was a *Brains Trust*, in which Marghanita Laski and Dr Grey Walters, an authority on the brain, took part.

As an adolescent I'd often been plagued with the alarming feeling that what was happening at a certain time I had seen happen before, with dire consequences. Sitting at a meal with my family I'd suddenly cry, "Stop, oh stop. this has all happened before and something terrible is going to happen". Once, visiting the home of a school-friend in Tankerness for the first time, I walked into her kitchen, which at once seemed familiar, and suddenly I knew that if I turned round I'd see an old man with a white moustache, wearing a hat, sitting on a chair. I did, and he was!

My sister remarked that on those occasions I became very pale and my eyes went black. I always felt a bit of a fool, for of course, fortunately, nothing drastic came to pass as I prophesied.

Now, listening to the *Brains Trust* on Stroma, I learned that this carry-on of mine was quite common and was called *déjà vu*. Dr Grey Walters said it was quite explicable, a statement which excited not only me, but also Miss Laski who'd often wondered about the experience. Dr Grey Walters said the sensation was caused by a slowing up of blood to the temples. I suppose that might have accounted, too, for my change in appearance.

The doubt that still remained in my mind, which I'd have liked to put to Dr Grey Walters, was — "Are you sure the slowing of the blood supply comes first, or is it the result of the alarming experience?"

What a difference it made to have an electric iron! Up

114

till then I had used my set of Mrs Potts' irons, an invaluable gift from a wedding guest. There were three Mrs Potts' irons — two of the same size and one smaller. They were heavy chunks of iron which you set on the top of the stove to heat. A composition handle clipped into the indentations in the top, and you used one till it became too cool, and then replaced it with a hot one. How light and how convenient the electric iron seemed after this!

I no longer had to hang the floor mats over the washing line and beat and beat with my cane clover-leaf carpet beater. My mother passed on her old Tellus vacuum cleaner, which very much resembled one of Dr Who's Daleks.

It was also much, much easier to touch switches than go through the performance — to me quite a nerve-wracking one — of lighting the Tilley lamp. I gave myself the most awful frights sometimes, by putting the light to the gauze mantle before it was hot enough, and then flames would shoot out of it in the most alarming way. Jimmy instructed me to apply the methylated spirit soaked heater twice, to make sure that when I screwed up the valve that sent the paraffin up to the mantle, it was at a temperature where it would ignite with a little pop, and not explode into a conflagration.

In other ways, however, we continued in a past era. Water for washing was collected off roofs and courtyards in large underground tanks from which it was piped to a sink in each house, the two sinks and bath in the wash-house and the three flushing lavatories. Our drinking water, which originated as a spring on the hill near the shop, had to be carried in from a tap at the station gate. The earliest containers for this job were clanking, black tin pitchers with lids and a handle over the top, by which you carried them. These were replaced with gaily coloured plastic water carriers.

The other summer I saw a replica of my first washing

machine being exhibited in a museum. It consisted of a metal tub on a stand. On top of the tub's lid was a handle which I pushed to and fro describing a semi-circle each time. Inside, a metal rod with a sort of paddle at the end swished the clothes about. The machine drained through a tap in the centre of the base, and the water flowed down the sloping, concrete floor and out through a drain in the middle. Anything needing more severe cleaning was rubbed up and down on a glass-fronted scrubbing board. There was one of those in the museum too.

Mrs Lamont had an even more ancient form of washing machine. It consisted of a copper cone with holes in it, at the end of a long pole. She manipulated this device by plunging it up and down in a bath full of washing. It was surely very effective, for my grandmother, a connoisseur of washing, described Mrs Lamont's flapping lines (having first hopefully and surprised, asked if they were my achievement), as "beautiful washing".

Mrs Lamont also took an interest in washing ability, for she used to ask me to endorse her opinion of the bachelor Donald's results — "My, but can't Donald put out a lovely washing — as good as any woman's?" It was not a field in which I had any ambition to compete, or on which I had the slightest wish or necessary amount of interest to make comment.

Neither did I worship the duster. One Hogmanay, Mrs Lamont enquired cheerily, "Well, is all the old year's dust out?"

The wicked rejoinder which I firmly bit back was, "Why, is there going to be a new kind in the New Year?"

Though I liked my surroundings to be neat, clean and tidy I was not always enthusiastic about carrying out the operations necessary to achieve this state of affairs.

No, what appealed to me were walks and picnics on fine days at any time of year.

Whenever Jimmy was free we'd pop some sandwiches and cakes and flasks of coffee into a bag, and set off to explore the island. After the depopulation left us with only the Manson family of four and the lighthouse folk, we felt we had the freedom of the whole island.

While the depopulation was going on I mourned the death of Stroma, but gradually I became aware that it was dead only humanly speaking. Life continued all over it.

When I came to Stroma I did not recognise the different kinds of sea-birds. Grey and white birds were all gulls to me. I'd never given birds a thought. Now, quite suddenly, I found myself wanting to know which was which and how they behaved and how they lived — in fact, all about them.

I also became aware of the life growing all over the island. I'd never before given wild plants other than a passing thought. Now I was longing to know their identities and something about them. It was like wakening up to a new world, full of interesting creatures and plants.

Every walk became a trail of discovery. Sometimes the binoculars were necessary, sometimes a magnifying glass, for I found that gazing into the world of a flower was a thrilling experience. The calyx of the sea-pink became a sheath of golden red, the minute green berries of the crowberry swelled roundly, a "mealiness" appeared on the leaves and stalks of the Scots primrose, and delicate stamens, so very fragile, were disclosed in violets. I can't tell you how enjoyable and fascinating life became!

We bought — I don't know how we afforded them — three bird books by T A Coward. These were *The Birds of the British Isles and their Eggs, Series 1 and 2* and *The Birds of the British Isles, Migration and Habits, Series 3.* For quick recognition we obtained Collins' *Pocket Guide to British Birds* by R S R Fitter and R A Richardson, and Collins' *Pocket Guide to Wild Flowers* by David McClintock and R S R Fitter. We never left home without the *Pocket Guides*, not

117

even when we went on leave to Orkney. I got to the stage of making sure our annual trips away from the island did not interfere with our bird and flower watching, and we left our leave till the last possible moment.

Incidentally, one time we left the island after being about a year on it, I wondered what would impress me most on the return to so-called civilisation. Well — it was a row of jars of boiled sweets on a shelf in a café in Wick. I couldn't take my eyes off them. They looked so pretty, like a collection of beautifully coloured jewels. The other thing we noticed was that we could not sleep in the silence of the guest house. We'd been used to a background pounding of engines.

On every walk I took a little notebook and scrawled down every interesting thing we saw, writing my notes up more carefully in a jotter in the evenings. I have four red covered jotters entitled "Walks on Stroma". From them I can recall many wonderful days in the island year.

We didn't need to go far in winter to bird watch. There were fine days when the sea hushed in to the shore in blue silken swells and still smooth pools among the rocks gleamed like polished mirrors. Down below the station were bared huge, flat rock tables where oyster-catchers, turnstones, ringed plovers and purple sandpipers feasted. There were no little pebbles here so I couldn't realise my ambition and see turnstones turn stones. Instead they flipped over tresses of sea-weed, like somebody flicking locks of hair in their search for tit-bits. Should we go too near, the oyster-catchers would rise in striking black and white formations and the other waders would flutter ahead of us like showers of silvery leaves. T A Coward tells of seeing the oyster-catchers dance. He described them in spring "trilling a nuptial song", but adds that another ornithologist, Professor J S Huxley claims that the dance is not always performed during courting, but at other times

118

too. I watched and watched for this and on 16 July saw the dance of the oyster-catchers.

They ran in a line, their orange bills open and held downwards, tri-i-i-lling passionately, their heads turning from side to side as they ran. In front of the line was a non-performer and, it seemed to me, that two of the others were out mainly to impress her. The two amorous birds, after the company had ceased to dance, pursued the object of their affection from rock to rock, and when they caught up with her, bowed their heads again and resumed trilling.

There were birds that completely mystified me when I first saw them in the winter-time. One was a grey and white gull with a little black spot on the side of its head. The black mark turned out to be all that remained of the completely black head seen in the summer on the black-headed gull.

The other was a pure white bird, barred and tipped with black. In the summer we had lain on the cliff-tops looking at it in a very different guise. It was the black guillemot who, in the summer, was all sooty black except for a large white patch on either wing. It paddled about with its red feet that looked as though they were made of red india rubber, and when it opened its bill to emit a high-pitched whistle, or to catch the little pinkish translucent eels it relished, revealed a bright red interior. I used to think it resembled a colourful clockwork toy. When we found two of its eggs in a deep rock crack and watched their progress, we found that when the young take flight, they are dressed in winter plumage.

Another, to my mind, toy-like bird was the puffin, with its huge, brightly coloured bill. Puffins lived in a warren of rabbit burrows, on a jagged cliff edge called the Kame of Kam. When we sat on the cliffs watching them, they whirred up and hovered beside us and did their human watching. It's a wonder nobody has thought of manufac-

119

turning clockwork black guillemots for the bath, or felt puffins for cuddling, but maybe I'm alone in thinking them toy-like.

One windy December day, when the low winter sun struck our eyes most uncomfortably as we headed westward on the cliff-tops, we changed course and went further inland. The first creature we saw was a sleepy little hedgehog out enjoying the touch of sunshine. We stroked his furry forehead — there's not much else one can do to show a hedgehog one likes him, and he closed his eyes and breathed steadily as though dropping off to sleep again.

After coming off watch at midnight one night, Mr James Allan was walking up the deserted road to his home, when he heard behind him a sound like somebody breathing heavily and with difficulty. For the first few times he ignored the noise, though he must have felt a little surprised, to say the least, to hear any such thing on that lonely road. After several hearings, he bravely turned round to investigate. The culprit — one small hedgehog!

The same day we met the hedgehog, we spotted a group of ducks on a loch at the low, west corner. To get near enough for identification, we had to get down and crawl — wet knees at once. What a beautiful, colourful sight was awaiting us — teal with rich chestnut heads, deep green patches outlined in yellow, and silver-grey bodies. White chested widgeon, with deep russet heads and a deep orangey-yellow band curving over the forehead, and silkily green-headed mallard drakes. The enchanted moments ended with a rising like a Peter Scott picture, accompanied by a sort of trembling, drumming whisper, the music of soft feathered wing-beats.

There was another piece of water we always approached with caution. It was a man-made loch on the west-side moorland. It had come into being because the Stroma men's hobby was sailing model yachts. There were already two lochs on the island, but the competitors wanted a larger, more weed-free expanse than they had. They erected a high, stout turf dyke — you could walk along the broad top — and soon the enclosure was filled with water provided by the rain and spray spouting over the west cliffs in winter storms.

One day in March we saw a beautiful picture here. On the still, blue water a gaggle of grey-lag geese were gliding. There were seven of them, soft, plump and pale grey with rich coral-orange bills.

Here, in season, huge jellied lumps of frog spawn swayed gently in the water, and sometimes the gorgeous sheldrakes rested.

Along the low east side, the solitary drab grey heron flew haughtily before us, like a sombre suited, hawky-faced dowager, taking umbrage at being disturbed.

Snow buntings, flitting to and fro like drifts of snow-flakes, fieldfares and redwings — colourful members of the thrush family — called in passing from their colder northern lands, and tiny gold-crested wrens, more like butterflies than birds, fluttered on and off garden walls, adding their high chirping song to the lonely, woebegone cry of the curlew, the cawing of the crows and the shrill pipe of alarm from the redshanks.

Spring came, and the hundred feet high cliffs of the island's west side were transformed. The litter of the past season — little mud-weed heaps left by kittiwakes and purply-green stains where shags had had their tangle nests, had been washed clean in the winter storms, and now, starting home-making afresh, the tenement dwellers had arrived. There were plump, irridescent, dark green shags on the basement steps, immaculate grey and white kitti-wakes on the first storey, common guillemots and razorbills like small head-waiters in their black and white tail-coated plumage on the next level, and gentle-eyed fulmar petrels at the top. Now the island's year was approaching its climax.

By the end of April sunny yellow celandines shone among the withered grasses and green-leaved scurvy grass, frothed with white flowers, cascaded down the cliffs.

We had to be careful where we trod. Birds' nests were everywhere. Lapwings laid in the fields, meadow pipits hid their eggs in tiny dried grass cups along the sides of ditches, and snipe rose with a breathtaking hoot of alarm from clutches in marshy places. Camouflaged most effectively were the brown eider ducks on their down-filled nests amongst the heather.

Near our hen house the dark brown Great Skua posted himself. As the long lines of white, blacktipped gannets glided past, he chose a victim and forced it into the sea, where in terror it regurgitated its food, which the Skua gobbled greedily.

The island was covered by a honey-scented carpet, richly patterned with wild flowers. Golden marsh marigolds and delicate, pale mauve lady's smocks turned the ditches into flower-filled troughs. Cushions of sea-pinks padded rocky ledges and grassy banks, and posies of primroses and violets clustered in sheltered hollows. Early marsh orchids and heath spotted orchids blossomed. There was tormentil, mountain everlasting, blue spring squills, scentless mayweed and heath bedstraw that lay like spoonfuls of some fluffy creamy confection among the heather. I have counted about seventy different flowers. I never picked the wild flowers, except the odd one for identification. I thought it a shame to cut short their lives. I don't mind cultivated flowers being used to cheer and comfort the ill and lonely, or sent as a romantic sign to a sweetheart, but the little wild things seem to me to belong to a different category.

I always found it rather surprising that oyster-catchers and ringed plovers chose bare stony patches for their nests, and most often lined the dent made for the purpose with tiny stones. It did not look at all comfortable, but of course was excellent camouflage.

One evening we took friends with their two year old daughter down to the west point. We'd chosen the most exciting time, for the eggs of herring gulls and greater black-backed gulls were cracking open all round us on the weed-covered cliff top. Fascinated, we watched the chicks struggle into the world. Later I heard of a child refusing to eat eggs after seeing one hatch. I hope our experience had no such result on our young guest.

The tenement west-cliff dwellers also had their families. Shags, their wings outstretched like black, tattered sails, guarded their young. Little kittiwakes filled their precarious cup-like homes, baby guillemots and razorbills dodged about and hid behind their parents' protective wings. Prettiest of all were the pale grey powder puff chicks of the fulmars.

As they all grew up and gradually departed, and the flowers withered and died, I used to say to Jimmy, "Oh I do hope they leave us to live through another year on Stroma", but the end arrived quite suddenly.

The Northern Lighthouse Board decided to make Stroma into a rock station. This would mean that the men would be two months on the island and one month at home at the shore station in Stromness, Orkney.

With some dismay we received the number of our house-to-be in Stromness. After all, Jimmy had been six years on Stroma.

During the Superintendent's last visit I had requested that when we were moved, would he please take into consideration that we'd like to have children. Stromness would fill the bill, but oh — Jimmy wouldn't be with me! The doctor who looked after us from Caithness had asked if we intended having a family, and made it clear that were I to become pregnant on the island, he'd whisk me away to "the other side". I was not leaving Jimmy and Paradise. We postponed having our family till we were geographically suitably placed.

The next thing that happened was that Jimmy was summoned to the phone. The call was from the Northern Lighthouse headquarters telling Jimmy to pack more securely than for crossing the Firth to Stromness. We were going further afield. "Could you let me know where we're going?" asked Jimmy. "There's a letter in the post", was the reply.

More anxious, but fully occupied, waiting. Nearly everything Jimmy had constructed — book cases, coffee table — had been made so that they could be dismantled for packing. He had also stored away all boxes in which our possessions had been sent when purchased.

At last the letter concerning our posting arrived. We were to proceed to Buchan Ness Lighthouse, Boddam, near Peterhead, Aberdeenshire.

Reluctantly, it was decided I precede Jimmy, and spend a few days with our disappointed families in Orkney, for they had been delighted at the first news — a transfer to Orkney.

And so I climbed the hill above the station for the last time, and took a last, long, tearful look at our first dear home, where we'd experienced so much happiness. I felt, and rightly so, that life would never be the same again.

The only consolations were that we'd been left on Stroma as long as possible — I was the last wife at the station — and James Simpson, a son of The Mains of Stroma, had bought the island, and begun to tame it. He and his wife and son came over and stayed for periods in the Nurse's house. He put cattle to graze, and planted oats

124

by his old home, The Mains. The cultivated patch looked incongruous, but was also the sign that Stroma was no longer only for the birds, the flowers and us. An era had ended. It was time for us to go.

Chapter Twelve

THE LIGHTHOUSE authorities had arranged that we and our belongings should cross by the *Pole Star* to Stromness. There we should transfer ourselves and things to the motor vessel *St Clair* which would transport us, taking approximately eight hours to do so, to Aberdeen. From there our goods and chattels had to be moved by lorry to Buchan Ness, Boddam.

Since I was such a wretched traveller, we decided to do the journey from Orkney by aeroplane — the quickest method, but one which I loathed as much as boat travel.

First of all I flew to Orkney from Wick, and amazed my fellow passengers by reassuring them that the foghorn bellowing from Noss Head Lighthouse nearby did not mean further delays by fog, like those inexplicable ones that had kept us sitting wearily for some considerable time at Wick airport. On Friday mornings — and that was the day

— foghorns were all blown to make sure they were functioning properly.

A few days after my arrival in Orkney, Jimmy crossed the Pentland Firth by *Pole Star*, as arranged, with all our possessions including our hens. Jimmy's mother had agreed to give them a home and promised that the ancient "Old White" whom we'd inherited from Donald would be allowed to live out her life-span.

We flew south to Aberdeen, and spent the night in a fairly comfortable hotel on Union Street. The food was very good, and somebody told us later that excellent beef was always served, for the proprietor was also a farmer who supplied his choicest products for the table. Mine host embarrassed us somewhat. Jimmy was, of course, travelling in lighthouse uniform, which this gentleman mistook for naval, and seemed to think such dress merited nods, winks and rather ribald jokes. We were thoroughly taken aback.

The next morning we caught a bus to Peterhead. The landscape of Buchan did not look much different from that of Orkney. There were slightly more treed patches, but on the whole it stretched flat and grassy from the roadside. There was no panorama of beautiful and interesting island shapes on the smooth grey sea. It stretched rather boringly and unadorned to the distant horizon.

Then, quite suddenly, from a hilltop we looked down on our home-to-be — a tall, white tower with a red band round its middle and its brood of small, flat-roofed, pure white buildings gathered round its base.

About a second before this scene claimed my attention I knew for sure that we were going to have a child — a new being conceived on our beloved Stroma. Like Peter Ustinov and his pride in knowing of his conception in, I think, Leningrad, this fact greatly pleased our son, Richard, when I informed him of it years later.

As was the way at lighthouses, we were welcomed and

entertained to tea by the Principal and his wife, Mr and Mrs McKellar, but not accepted by their ultra nervous poodle.

We met the First Assistant, David Leslie, his slim, pretty dark-haired wife and their three young children. The Principal Keeper's house was at right angles to the rest of the complex, and was in a separate block which contained also the oil store, a work-shop and the engine room. Davy's house, containing a room for the Occasional Keeper with a door opening to the outside, was to the left of the tower and opposite it, on the other side of a concreted, rectangular courtyard and forming the third side of the rectangle, was our house. We again had four rooms, two on either side of the central lobby which terminated in a proper bathroom — what luxury!

Everything had been left spotlessly clean, the inside of cupboards distempered pure white. A huge Wellstood cooker warmed the kitchen. There was a porcelain sink and a small alcove at one end. But, oh dear, the varnished wallpaper half way up the kitchen and lobby walls! "That must be removed", we agreed, and in the lull, while waiting for our belongings to arrive from Aberdeen docks, we painted on varnish remover and scraped and scraped and scraped — me in my going-away suit, the skirt of which somehow got too near to the Wellstood fire door, and had an unrescuable hole burnt in it, much to my chagrin.

We were again on an island, but this time one we could walk round in about ten minutes. The only birds to be seen were herring gulls and the occasional shag. People walked their dogs round the wall that enclosed the lighthouse complex, for the island was joined to the village of Boddam by a black, wooden bridge.

We went for a walk and tried to get off streets. But here

there were notices announting PRIVATE, and when at last we found a free bit of heathery moor, it ended in a rubbish dump. How homesick we were for Stroma!

Neither clearly, cold-bloodedly, nor decisively, but in a slow befuddled way, it came to me that I had to become reconciled to an entire change of existence, and had somehow to find completely different interests.

Jimmy, of a more gregarious nature than I, came home from the village one day with news of a "Tatties and Herrin'" evening in the Church Hall. He wanted to go, though neither of us knew what kind of entertainment this was to be.

It was a cold, dark winter's night when we made our way to the hall adjoining the village Church of Scotland. Inside all was warm, well-lit and welcoming. Mrs Sellars, who remained a friend ever after, invited us to sit beside her and her husband. Boiled salt herring and boiled potatoes all piping hot were served — but no cutlery. The tradition was to eat with the fingers, and just as chips taste best from the paper "poke" straight out of the chip shop, so "tatties and herrin'" taste delicious eaten with the fingers. After the feast, basins of warm water and towels were passed round so that we could wash our hands.

After that the hall was cleared of tables, and made ready for an evening of hilarious, sometimes boisterous, games, for example an energetic "Grand Old Duke of York", and the passing round of a sack containing all sorts of weird garments. Two boys with piano accordions provided the music. When the music stopped the person in possession of the sack had to haul out a garment and dress in it, usually looking quite ridiculous as a result. One lady near me moaned gently, "I bet I get Johnny Noble's drawers, I always do". And she did!

I remarked to my partner in one game that I noticed

they didn't have any dances. He explained that some of the church members would not allow dancing in their hall. He, like me, could see little more reverence about the games we were playing.

Eventually I found out about the "Tatties and Herrin'" evenings of the past — probably, but I can't be certain of this, how they originated.

The "Tatties and Herrin'" was one of a series of festivities that took place when there was a wedding in Boddam. I was fascinated to learn of the wedding procedures in the past.

Courting was conducted as far as possible in secret, and to many people the intimation that there was to be a wedding came as a great surprise.

About a fortnight before the wedding the names of bride and groom were handed to the registrar and arrangements were made to have the banns proclaimed in the church in Peterhead. This proclamation was known as "being cried".

On the night after those arrangements had been made the first festivity was held. This was called "The Buiken Pairty", and took place in the home of the bride-to-be. Close friends and relatives were invited to have tea, sometimes followed by parlour games.

The next day the couple, with their parents, went to Peterhead for a shopping expedition. At one time they walked to town. Later they took a horse-drawn bus. At a very early date it is thought that those expeditions were made by boat, but that this method of transport was given up after a boating accident in which a boat capsized, and several people were drowned.

The fathers and bridegroom saw to the buying of furniture, and the bridegroom was also expected to give the bride, the two bridesmaids — "the maidens", his mother and his mother-in-law material for their wedding dresses. The bride had to provide white shirts for the groom and both his best men — "the gweedmen".

The bride and one of her maidens and the groom and a gweedman invited the guests to the wedding during the fortnight preceding it. This was known as the "biddin'" of the guests. When families were large only the two oldest members were invited.

The second festivity took place on the eve of the wedding. It was called the "decoration o' the Hoose". Most of the heavier pieces of furniture were previously installed but portable objects had still to be brought in. An aunt of the bride and an aunt of the groom took their places in the empty house to receive the items of furnishing. The bride was not permitted to see her new home till after the wedding.

The first object was the bolster borne in by the groom, followed by his "gweedmen" carrying a pillow each. As the groom crossed the threshold one of the aunts broke a plate or a bowl for luck.

When the groom had handed over his bolster he quickly disappeared and went into hiding for the night. Sometimes the bride joined him, for they both tried to keep out of the way and miss the ritual known as "feet washin'".

Into a tub in the bride's house was put a mixture of tar, blacklead, feathers and treacle or syrup, and if the couple were unfortunate enough to be caught, their feet were "washed" in this concoction.

Early on the morning of the wedding day the two best men hung flags and bunting across the street from the bride's home. Then the groom's family and the bride's family in their respective homes entertained aunts and uncles to breakfast, which consisted of boiled salt fish and oatcakes.

After this, the married female relatives went to the new house to make up the beds, and then, joined by other married women friends, repaired to the village hall where they prepared the long tables for the wedding feast. In early days there were two feasts, one about four in the afternoon and a later one at perhaps eight in the evening.

When either the school bell or the kirk bell rang out, the bride, supported on either side by the gweedmen and followed by her friends lined up in twos, made her way to the church or hall, depending on where the ceremony was to take place.

Shortly after this the bridegroom, with a maiden on each arm and followed by his friends, arrived for the ceremony.

The bridal party lined up in front of the minister, who conducted the ceremony amid silence. There was no singing and no floral decorations.

If the marriage took place in the church, her oldest aunt on her mother's side, met the bride on her entering the hall and, placing a fine handkerchief on the part of her head which showed in front of her bonnet, broke a piece of fruit cake over her to wish her life-long plenty. The bride then took her place at the table, and, when seated, her bonnet was removed by the same aunt who had broken the cake.

Everybody then tucked in to the fare provided, thick slices of bread, lumps of cheese, butter, jam and all sorts of fancy cakes and biscuits. There was no wedding cake, but slices of fruit cake appeared on plates when it became more common.

When there were two feasts, during the interval between them, most of the guests visited the bride and groom in their new home and drank their health. Other visits were paid and people also took walks till it was time for the second feast. After it, the furniture was cleared away to make room for games and dancing.

When bed-time came the young people gathered once

more at the new house for "The Beddin'". Amidst much hilarity the bride and groom were helped to bed. The bride threw her stocking from the bed and whoever caught it was supposed to be the next to marry.

The following night came the second and last festivity, when the gweedmen and the maidens invited close friends for "Tatties and Herrin'". Salt herring, boiled on top of potatoes in their jackets were served, followed by tea and fancy cakes and biscuits.

On the Sabbath morning after the wedding the ritual came to an end. The new wife dutifully laid out her new husband's "Sabbath day claes". The two gweedmen accompanied the couple to church for "the Kirkin'". The maidens, who had stayed with the bride and groom since the wedding and helped in the house, now performed their final task — they cooked the dinner.

Chapter Thirteen

AT THE lighthouse, life went on much as it had done in
Stroma. Watch was kept for fog by day and night, in
addition to the normal station duties and, from sunset to
sunrise, the light had to be attended. Every forty-five
minutes the man on watch wound up the clockwork
mechanism, which brought the heavy metal weight to the
top of the never ending chain that dangled almost the
entire length of the tower. The great, glittering lens
revolved — this time on a bath of mercury, and not on
rollers as in Stroma — and the light flashed once in every
five seconds.

A large, black cat began persistently to visit us, and it
became apparent he had come to stay. We named him
"Kipling", because of that writer's story *The Cat who
Walked by Himself*. Nobody thought of telling us that he had
belonged to our predecessors and had escaped during their

packing. It turned out they had called him "Blackie". Kipling, as we knew him, would disappear for weeks on end, and return dirty and smelly, with tattered ears and other war wounds.

Days and nights passed in a peaceful, orderly way, except for those occasions when a strong south-east wind coincided with the high tides just after a full moon. Our house was nearest to the sea, and I, feeling uneasy, used to press my ear to the darkened panes and try to judge the whereabouts of the sea. It was in such conditions that, seven years earlier, two waves had collided, becoming a "doubler", crashed through the lighthouse wall, swept an Occasional Keeper along until he managed to grab a ladder lashed to a wall, and flooded what was now our house. Fear of living close to the sea was new to me — another unwelcome change from life on Stroma.

However, the biggest difference between Stroma and Buchan Ness was in being able to walk across a bridge, about fifty yards in length, and come into contact with other people.

The replacement of that wooden bridge by a concrete structure was to give me perhaps the most miserable few weeks I had ever spent.

Because of my great age — thirty-two — I was put under the care of a specialist gynaecologist. A gale blew up and we had been left with only a cat-walk on which to cross to the mainland. I paid my usual monthly visit to the cottage hospital in Peterhead, and the specialist decided our baby was about to arrive that day. He told me not to return to the lighthouse, not even for my suitcase, because if events occurred as hastily as he thought they would, it would not be possible (because of lack of bridge) to send an ambulance to the island for me. Jimmy was to take me to the large maternity hospital in our nearest city, Aberdeen.

Now, I had read and re-read Dr Winifred de Kok's

excellent book *Your Baby and You*, and had become convinced that the birth of a child was to be one of the greatest experiences one could ever have. So it came as a shock to be greeted by a stony-faced nurse who "humphed" bad-temperedly, and passed no other remark, when I happily informed her that the specialist thought our baby would arrive that night. Jimmy left me prostrate on a hard, high trolley in a terrifyingly instrumented room.

Things improved. I was put to bed in a pleasant room containing two beds and attended by pleasant friendly people. However, I was left there only for a day or two, then taken into an enormous ward with many beds. I tried to talk with the person in the next bed, to be answered by an ill-mannered grunt. The other inmates kept on asking "When are they going to start you off?" What was this? No word of this in Dr Winifred de Kok.

A doctor plumped down by my bedside with a sheaf of papers. He said he was going to ask me a few questions.

Well, I tried to comply, but when it came to, "How many sanitary towels did you use?" — a subject with which I had happily had no contact for the past nine months — I hesitated. "Come on, come on", urged my questioner impatiently, adding testily, "You *must* know that". No word about this sort of treatment in Dr W de Kok!

While on the same disagreeable topic, one patient asked if she could have more sanitary towels, to be snapped at, "You wouldn't use so many if you had to pay for them". The lady was made of sterner stuff than I, "Oh but I *am* paying for them. My husband buys his stamp for this".

Then she too was "started off". A drip was set up and left in the charge of two youngsters, who immediately started discussing what their instructions really meant.

"I'd rather you asked and made sure", protested the victim.

"Oh we know what we're doing all right", came the rejoinder. Time passed and a doctor arrived on the scene to point out that they had entirely misunderstood the instructions and were not administering the treatment correctly.

Thoroughly alarmed and upset by my surroundings, I anxiously asked a visiting doctor if there was any intention of "starting me off", explaining to him that I had only been put there because of lack of a bridge — there was nothing wrong and I wanted a natural birth. He did mutter a few words of reassurance, but the minute he was through the door, the accompanying staff nurse returned, spitting like a wild cat. "How dare you suggest we're starting off without cause etc, etc" — which I had not done.

At last a top person made a round, looked at me and said, "Wouldn't you rather wait at home?" Would I rather! Immediately I phoned Jimmy, "Come and take me out of this place at once".

However, when I got home, the local district nurse — a simply wonderful person — called. I had developed dangerously high blood pressure — little wonder — and should not have been allowed out of hospital.

Next day, doped so that I didn't much care what happened any more, I was carried across the cat-walk on a stretcher, to a waiting ambulance. This time the local doctor had arranged for me to have a private room.

Labour was induced by breaking the waters. Our son, Richard, was born successfully. I won't bore you with all the unpleasantness of the post-natal period in "that place", as Mrs Lamont would have called it. Suffice it to say I vowed I would never ever return thither, and two years later, our daughter arrived delightfully in the small cottage hospital in Peterhead, where everybody was not only very efficient, but also very pleasant, and the experience lived up to expectations.

While in hospital to have our daughter, I had no worries about my little son, Richard, for when his father came to visit, Richard was taken into the kind and loving care of the Principal Keeper of that time, Mr Kenneth Macgillivray, his wife — our dear "Nan" — and their young but grown-up family.

While waiting for our daughter's arrival, Jimmy brought me a book from the library entitled *My First Hundred Years* by an archaeologist, Margaret Murray. In this book I came across the information that there had been a saint called Katherine, who was believed to care for warning lights for sailors. "There's the name for the daughter of a lightkeeper", I said to Jimmy, and so when our dear daughter arrived she was duly named Katherine.

Chapter Fourteen

WE HAD now come to the phase of the perambulator, and could walk only where a pram could be wheeled.

The kindly Boddam folk peeped into our pram, remarked, "My, isn't he keen?" and deposited some silver coins on the pillow, as "lucky pennies". And when the occupant grew bigger, the old men, who always greeted us cheerily from the granite "seaties", often had a sweet or some chocolate for him.

The "seaties" — benches of pink granite — had been erected, I discovered, by Lord Aberdeen who became Prime Minister in 1852. In 1840, this gentleman had built a marine villa on the cliff-tops to the south of the village, and so enjoyed watching the fishing fleets sail by, that he had the "seaties" put up along the sea front for the women to sit on and enjoy the sight too.

We walked along the quiet streets of the village, and explored the little labyrinths that lay off them.

A shopping expedition was more like calling on friends. Cottages were used as shops, which added to the feeling that one was visiting. I'm sure that, as elsewhere, profit and loss mattered, but Janet, Sophia and Mrs Sutherland seemed to be more interested in seeing you than in your being a prospective customer. At Janet's and Sophia's you could buy drapery goods, knitting wool and little nick-nacks often bearing the message "Present from Boddam" and very frequently depicting Buchan Ness lighthouse. Mrs Sutherland mainly sold groceries. The Post Office had a shop department too, and there it was possible to buy a cake baked by the Postmaster's father.

At the harbour, where we could watch stones plop satisfactorily into the water, or, more rarely, skip over the surface for mother was no expert at this art, two boats came in with crabs and lobsters for the little sea-food factory nearby.

I was amazed when my Boddam friends and my researches spoke of Boddam as a busy fishing port. About 1880 there had been 151 boats, 476 fishermen and over a thousand people employed in the fishing industry.

For Boddam, the seasons were marked by the kind of fish to be sought. From September till Candlemas cod were caught. From March to July haddock arrived, and all was industry and bustle on the Boddam shore, for this fish was so carefully processed there that it brought renown to the village. The haddocks were split, washed and salted and stacked on the beach in heaps. Then they were spread out on scrupulously clean rocks to dry. Every night they were gathered again into heaps and every morning were spread out again. At last, when sufficiently dry, they were stored at home until they were smoked over peat fires to give them the colour and flavour that made them so popular in the market place.

The summer's sea crop, however, filled Boddam's cornucopia. The shoals of herring swam in their thousands into eager, waiting nets. On shore, everything was made ready to receive the silver harvest. The eleven curing yards were fully staffed with crews of fisher girls. Each crew consisted of two "gutters" and a "packer". The gutters bandaged fully the thumb and forefingers of each hand with yellow calico tied with cotton. The packer rolled up every finger over the tips and half-way down. Thus prepared, each crew stood behind five tubs. Mrs John Noble Stephen showed me the small sharp, wooden-handled knife she had used when, in her oilskin pleated skirt with breast-high bib, knee-length leather boots and headsquare, she had earned her living by gutting the herring. She told me, too, the whole process carried out when the farmers' carts, summoned by a flag, had trans-ported the fish from shore to yard.

First, as the herring were emptied into oblong boxes called "farlans", a cooper sprinkled them with salt. The girls gutted at the rate of fifty-eight fish a minute, and tossed each fish into one of the five tubs, depending on its size. There were "dead small", matties' nine and a half inches long, and, bigger than that, "mattie full", "full", and "large full". As the season came to its close there were "spent", meaning spawned herring.

When the tubs were full, the crew took them to what was called the "roosin'" tub, where the packer poured salt on the fish and mixed and tumbled them about in the salt. Mrs Stephen showed me, by arranging matchsticks on the table, how the fish were then packed firmly into the barrels layer about with salt.

Mrs Stephen's working day sometimes lasted from 6 am

141

to past midnight, out in the unsheltered curing yard, earning 3d an hour.

The coopers "put on the heads" and the barrels were left for ten days. The fish settled and had to be topped up after the first night they were packed, and again ten days later. This final filling up was done by the coopers boring a hole about a quarter of the way up the sides of the barrels, and through this opening draining off the salt pickle. The "heads" were again removed, the barrels filled to the top with more fish and salt, heads fastened down, the salt pickle poured back through the hole and a bung pushed into position.

Next came the test by the fishery officer to see if the herrings were properly processed and good. This officer's judgement depended primarily on his taste buds for, pointing to barrels here and there in the "parcel of herrings", he ordered that they be opened, some at the top, some at the bottom. Choosing a herring from each opened barrel, he took a bite out of its back. If it tasted to his satisfaction, was firm to the touch and had bright, silvery scales, he granted the seal of approval. Then each barrel could be branded with a design known as the Crown Brand, and was thus guaranteed to keep in any climate for twelve months.

The branding procedure was in operation from 1808 to 1950, and was applicable only to Scottish Fisheries.

Fishery officers were at times not at all popular, and in some places had to carry blue-painted police type batons with which to fend off attack. No wonder fisher folk became enraged if, at the end of their intensive labour, their product did not pass the test.

Boddam's barrels of herring were sold far and near. Mr Pat Sellar told me how his grandfather's schooner, *The Industry*, would sail to the Baltic, laden with branded

142

herring, and return, full of oak, to build more boats. There were at one time five boatbuilding yards in the village. Pat Sellar's grandfather sounded an enterprising man. When he was at sea, he had with him two pigeons, one of which flew home to report where he'd shot his nets, while the other was dispatched to the curing yard with the amount of his catch. His wife ground her mustard seed with the cannonball of a French press gang ship which had chased some of the Boddam boats.

Fishermen were expected to play their part in the community. If a boat was to be launched or hauled up, a notice appeared on a board, and every man with a share in a boat or in a boat's net had to turn up and do his bit. The only excuse accepted was illness, and if there was not that reason, then the absentee was fined.

By 1900 the boom in Boddam's fishing industry was over. In 1928, a newspaperman talking of the decline of the fishing industry in the North East villages, stated, "Nowhere, however is the decline more pronounced or the distress more acute than at Boddam". The trawler had arrived on the scene and filched the sea's plenty from the inshore fishermen. A dozen motor-engined boats still tried to make a living, but it was proving impossible. The day's average catch was one or two boxes of codlings for which they might get about 30/- out of which they had to cover their expenses.

Peter Anson, visiting the village in 1930, found it "silent and deserted, with grass growing on the piers of its harbour built half a century ago or more to accommodate the fleet of boats which filled it". At the time of his visit fifteen line boats went small line fishing and the old men "who seem to belong to another age", caught lobsters and crabs for a living. This story fills me with sadness.

One of the few permanent sea-faring things about the village was the stout granite-built lighthouse tower on

143

Buchan Ness. It had come into being in 1827, but only after much fuss and bother. In 1790, the writer of the Statistical Account suggested that a lighthouse be built on Stirling Hill. The Boddam folk agreed with him that the hill was a useful landmark but, because of its height, a lighthouse there would not be seen in fog.

Petitions by "merchants, shipowners, shipmasters and others interested in shipping", were sent to the Northern Lighthouse Board on two occasions before it was persuaded to build a lighthouse. The petitioners were concerned about the number of shipwrecks on the Buchan coast — twenty between November 1816 and March 1819 — one of which, the sloop *Marchioness of Huntly*, was wrecked at Boddam itself in 1817.

Robert Robertson, who owned the island the Yards of Boddam, as Buchan Ness was then called, was very careful to safeguard the rights of the fisherfolk when he sold the land to the Commissioners of Northern Lights. The fishermen were to retain the right to haul their boats up on the island's shore and on the beach opposite on the mainland. They were also to be allowed to continue to dry fish on the rocks that encircled the island.

The foghorn did not appear on the rocks outside the lighthouse walls till 1904. One elderly lady, Mrs Isy Buchan, recalled how, as a child, she and friends used to station themselves behind the lighthouse when the fog rolled in, and beat tin basins with spoons to warn boats off the rocks. Mrs Buchan claimed the horn was blown on 10 December 1904 to celebrate a wedding in her family. Another Boddam friend was of the opinion that those first blasts were in honour of a relative's arrival in this world.

I never heard Mrs Buchan referred to as anything but Isy "Don". She belonged to a family of Cordiners who had Don as their "tee" name. One of our Occasional Keepers was Jimmy "Pith". His surname was Stephen but the

144

family were all called the "Piths". John Noble Stephen was called Johnny Noble and George Cameron Cordiner called George Cameron. Before my time, there had been "Bell's Peter", "Grocer's Jimmy" and "Jinty's Jock". There were so many people with the same surname that the "tee" names were essential. In one class at school there had been thirteen Bobby Stephens. To distinguish between them the teacher referred to each one by a number.

It would be interesting to know what the original Boddamers were called. In the 1843 Statistical Account it is stated that it was here that William of Orange had planted a settlement of Dutch fishermen. That would have been in the eighteenth century. The same writer of 1843 remarked that the inhabitants of his time married young, between the ages of eighteen and twenty, produced large families and lived to a good ripe age. I found them, in the twentieth century, to be kind, homely folk who helped to make pleasant my stay at Buchan Ness.

Chapter Fifteen

BODDAM fishermen so had the sea in their blood that even in their leisure hours they built and sailed boats — this time model ones. The adult men raced their boats, but each boat competed in the name of a son or other young relative. I used to think expectant fathers in Boddam must have been extra anxious before the birth of their progeny, hoping desperately for a male heir for whom to race a "boatie".

In our time, a pleasant day in summer, we all made our way up Stirling Hill behind the village to the Den Dam, a reservoir initially dammed for a granite polishing works near Stirling Village. This business closed down during our time in Boddam.

On the isolated loch the men raced their model yachts, passed from generation to generation.

This was a very different scene from those of the past. I

don't know when "The Sailin' o' the Shippies" started, but in the early days it took place as part of Boddam's Christmas celebrations, which did not take place on 25 December but on 5 January, known as "Aul Eel" — I suppose meaning Old Yule.

Often, at that time of year, the dam had ice on it, and before the fathers and sons could launch their yachts they had to break up the ice. Some supporters picnicked on the chilly banks while the racing went on.

It requires considerable knowledge and skill to sail boats successfully on the Den Dam. Jimmy and Richard have tried with a model made by my grandfather, and so far they have not got the hang of it. No doubt it is a matter of pride for the competitors to do well in their races, but no matter what the results every little boy gets his prize. In early times they were given shirts, stockings or scarves at the dam. Later they had to wait till the "Boatie Social" held early in the New Year and the gifts became, shall we say, more frivolous, taking the form of torches, pencil cases and the like. When Richard and I accompanied our friend Barbara to a very noisy children's party in the hall during the Christmas holidays one little boy near us proudly sported a plastic Noddy house as his winnings. Utilitarianism had gone by the board as have the accompanying rituals associated with the Den Dam outing.

By the time our Occasional Keeper, Alfie, took part, the sailing had been changed to New Year's Day, as the school holidays no longer included 5 January. He recalled a horse-drawn lorry bearing the boaties and a barrel of apples heading a procession to the Den Dam. Music was provided by a flute band, which led the fisherman committee, followed by everybody else.

He didn't tell of any other festivities on the day, but certainly before that, after the morning at the Dam and a welcome tuck-in on returning home to such fare as broth, beef and dumpling, the Boddam folk spent a sociable day.

There was a flat, grassy place known as the Factory Park where herring nets could be spread out to dry. There sports of various kinds were organised. The menfolk, blindfolded, tried to steer wheelbarrows to and round a pole and back to the starting point. They also attempted to climb a mast which had been greased at the top and erected with a currant loaf or fruit cake, to be retrieved by anyone who succeeded in reaching it. The women shied objects at "Sally Watt", the Boddam name for the traditional Aunt Sally of the fairground.

As darkness fell, people hurried home to get dressed for the "Ran Dan", or "Christmas Surree" (soirée). Before Boddam had a hall this celebration was held in a curing yard.

Long tables were set with plates of fancy cakes and biscuits, and cups were filled from shining brass kettles, each bearing a distinguishing coloured ribbon so that its rightful owner could claim it again.

After the feast, there was a concert at which the chairman had the sometimes difficult task of recounting the memorable events of the village's past year. I remember Peter "Don", in our time, puzzling his brains to gather material about village events and put it into verse form to recite at what was by then known as "The Boatie Social". Various other artistes gave of their best. The performances over, the hall was cleared for polkas, reels, schottisches, strip-the-willow and various other dances, and the company danced the night away.

Sad to say rowdyism crept in through the years and the more staid village inhabitants came to disapprove of the goings-on at the Ran Dan.

Really, up till this happened, the Aul Eel Day revels were the more civilised of Boddam's activities at this time of year. The previous evening was taken up with all sorts of ploys, the victims of which claim my late twentieth century sympathy. The poor fisherman who'd had the smallest catch that day had a "Kyarlin" attached to his chimney. This was the figure of an old woman made of a broomstick clothed in some elderly lady's garments. Clothes poles were dislodged and thrown about, boats were removed from the harbour and stranded inland, henhouses from nearby farms were transported to the harbour, and squawking fowls were pushed down chimneys to the distress of the locked-in inhabitants.

The only old Christmas custom we came across was when Marella, Alfie's little girl, who was about the same age as Richard, visited us on Hogmanay and announced on leaving that she was going home for "Santy is comin'". Richard immediately asked in amazement, "He's coming again?" We had to think quickly and explain that it was only to children in the village he came at Hogmanay. Everybody else got their presents on Christmas Day. Stockings in Boddam had been hung up on New Year's Eve from at least the 1870s.

A writer friend, Miss Kathleen Macleod, who lived in Boddam, had collected from old people long before my time, the details of the Christmas and wedding customs. After she died, another acquaintance let me see Miss Macleod's pieces; both of which greatly added to what I was told about Boddam. Miss Macleod, who was an invalid, had ceased to write when I met her. She had published several book-length stories and gave me a book she'd written about Wolf Cubs, to keep for Richard. She'd also had many short stories published in *The People's Friend*, but told me she preferred the large canvas of a book to the limited area of the short story or article. She urged me to keep on writing. "Get paper and pencil and plenty of stamps," she said, "and keep at it." But at that time I was so involved with my children I felt I was doing enough creating, without taking on any more.

149

Chapter Sixteen

WITH TWO young children, and Jimmy's periods on duty,
it was not possible for me to join in organised village
activities and so become acquainted with more people.
The agony columns all advise joining classes and clubs in
order to make friends. I've found on the few occasions I've
tried to follow this advice that everybody attending the
class or club was there with his or her already established
chums with the result that I felt more lonely than ever. But
that sort of thing came much later than my life as a lightkeeper's wife, when I experienced no loneliness.

At Buchan Ness, Mr McKellar, our Principal Keeper,
retired, and his replacement, Mr Kenneth Macgillivray,
his wife and teenage son, Kenneth, arrived at the lighthouse. They also had two young adult daughters who came
home on holiday — and all showed interest in and affection
for our Katherine and Richard as well as holding out the
hand of friendship to us.

Mrs Macgillivray became "Nan" to us. Her sense of humour and wisdom about life I greatly appreciated. I often think of some of her sayings — she believed that "Heredity is the rock on which everything breaks". Somebody said she'd come to the end of her tether. "Ah well," said Nan, "she'll just have to tie a knot and hang on." Looking far into the future I said to her once, "How terrible it must be when the children leave home."

"Even the eagle breaks up her nest," said Nan.

Nan and her student daughter, Catherine, enjoyed with me firstly the company of Richard and later the babyhood of Katherine, and, as I mentioned before, took care of Richard and kept him occupied and happy when Jimmy came to visit me in hospital on the birth of Katherine. Richard, happily trotting round the station with his father, was very fond too of "Mr Milly", as he called Mr Macgillivray.

There were some unusual aspects to being a child at a lighthouse. I don't suppose there are many little boys who waken to a bell summoning their fathers to work in the middle of the night. Richard often did, and cheerfully padded through to the kitchen to get a couple of digestive biscuits sandwiched together with butter, before seeing Jimmy off to go on watch. Then, quite satisfied with life, he'd quietly return to bed and sleep the rest of the night. I heard from Jimmy of those nocturnal treats only in the morning, for Richard never disturbed me or the baby, Katherine.

As parents, we were a pair of novices. We never thought about our children needing the companionship of their peers. I was surprised when a Boddam friend remarked that Richard wasn't allowed to "run out about" like "ither bairns". Well, for one thing we were over on the island away from other children, where he was blissfully happy romping out on the big expanse of grass where we hung our washing, or playing in a little fenced-in enclosure

151

by the side of our house, at first by himself, later with Katherine. We'd never thought about gregarious needs.

On two occasions when we did come in contact with "ither bairns" the result was not encouraging. One day I'd left Richard and the pram with Katherine in it outside Sophia's. When I came out, it was to put to flight a gang of little boys, who'd surrounded and set about teasing him. He was too terrified to move or protest. "They would not go away though I said 'shoo'," he declared.

The other incident ended in near disaster. A new Second Assistant had replaced David Leslie. His daughter, aged six or seven, wanted to take Richard out to play — I presumed within the confines of the station walls. Very shortly she returned to say he'd fallen over the cliff. My heart pounding I rushed out with her — there was Richard clinging on half way down the ash covered rubbish dump. Fortunately two bigger children on the beach below volunteered to climb up and rescue him.

Richard and Katherine preferred the fun and games provided by two new adult friends of ours — their adored "Uncle" Willie and Cecilia, a daughter of our doctor's locum, who took a great interest and played with the children and helped me with them.

Jimmy, when he was free on the right evening, went to the Camera Club in Peterhead, and there made friends with Willie. It was at this club, too, that he met another friend-to-be, Frank. Frank's wife, Margaret, had her baby daughter a month after I had mine, and both we and our little girls became life-long friends.

"Uncle" Willie, to everybody's great delight, spent his Wednesday half-holidays with us, and then in the summer he took us on a tour by car for a day's outing. We'd set off in the morning, drive through the countryside to a nice hotel, where we'd have coffee. Then on we'd go, perhaps visiting interesting churches, graves and ruins as we proceeded. Lunch would have been booked at some fine hostelry. One such outing I well remember, because of its aftermath. We visited Cullen House, home of the Seafields. I'd read that Cullen House was haunted, and felt uneasy and fearful throughout the visit. Not even afternoon tea in the huge kitchen, agleam with glowing copper utensils, and displaying glorious Van Dyck paintings, could take my thoughts out of their ghostly rut.

In one room of family portraits a man stared out at me. I couldn't take my eyes off him, and as I bore his penetrating gaze the thought, "Why, he's mad", entered my mind. When the guide came to talk of this portrait he told how this Earl of Seafield took fits of madness. When he felt one coming on he'd instruct his manservant to lock him in his room, and not release him till he let him know the madness had passed. Unfortunately, on one occasion, the man-servant opened the door before his master had given the word, and paid for his action with his immediate death. It was the spirit of this mad earl that was said to haunt the house. I couldn't get away quick enough.

We then ended our evening with a huge high tea at a pleasant guest house in the country.

Too much excitement? Too much food? Fatigue after a long day's driving about? I don't know, but I spent one of the most uncomfortable nights I've ever known, with the mad Earl of Seafield's face swimming before me every time I closed my eyes.

An outing with all our Camera Club friends took place when the club held a dinner in a Fraserburgh hotel. After the meal, the entertainment was a film show by one of the members. The subject was his summer holiday on the Continent, so we saw churches, castles and important buildings all over western Europe, each one resembling the next, in that standing stoutly in front of every edifice was the film maker's rather well-built wife. One disastrous section of the film was where it had been shot through the windows of a travelling coach. Frank closed his eyes for he feared he'd be sea-sick.

Company at home was no longer limited to lighthouse personnel. Indeed at Buchan Ness it was only at coffee-times, when the men took a break in the morning, that we had the company of Occasional Keepers and artificers from Edinburgh when they made their rounds. The latter were lodged in the village. My time of keeping lodgers had passed.

We also now took part in the tourist trade. Crowds of people came to be shown over the station. One afternoon Jimmy was being guide to visitors up the tower when I had an alarming caller. He was a boy of twelve or so, supported by friends and streaming blood from a hand on which was a nearly severed thumb.

Quickly I asked a visitor about to go up the tower, 150 stone steps, to tell Jimmy that a child — not his own — was badly injured and to please come at once. Once the boy was seated in the kitchen I phoned our doctor, who was fortunately available. In minutes he was with us, and the considerable wound was held under the running tap and then stitched. Not a whimper from that brave boy! He'd fallen on the rocks while holding a glass bottle. He was staying in Boddam School at a school holiday camp, and later that day his teachers came to thank us for helping. We remarked on the boy's courage. "They breed them tough in Greenock", said the teacher with a smile.

Children often played on the rocks round the lighthouse and went swimming in a big natural, tide-washed pool, among the rocks which was known as "The Washer". In our time a project was set going to make sure The Washer was really as hygienic and safe as everybody had always thought. Some medical people voiced their doubts about it.

One day one of the children on the rocks — a boy — appeared at the lighthouse to inform the keepers that he'd just seen a man being carried past on the tide. They checked speedily, and there was a figure in what they thought was a Mae West jacket, floating helplessly past on the ebbing sea. The alarm was raised and Peterhead life-boat alerted, but at once our Occasional Keeper, Alfie Buchan and his son, unable to get their motor boat out of the completely ebbed dry harbour, carried a little skiff which they had to the water, and rowing with might and main raced after the man and rescued him. He'd been canoeing some miles down the coast, capsized and kept himself afloat by clinging to a float out of the canoe. On rescue he was just about to lose his hold on his float.

Other changes that took place in our life included my ceasing to bake so much. I didn't have much time with two little children to look after, and there was the novelty of a baker's van that came every week day. Cakes and biscuits, milk and newspapers, arriving at the door, seemed at first to belong to the realms of magic.

Then, too, we could all pile into our old car and go picnicking in that, to us, alien surrounding of trees, visit beaches and gather pretty shells and build sand castles, swing in playparks or see the bright lights in nearby towns.

Jimmy and I were delighted with our two new little companions whom we treated as just that.

Five years passed quickly — five years of spending most of our time with Katherine and Richard, and enjoying the kindness, companionship and stories of the Boddam friends who welcomed us amongst them.

Now we felt sure our next posting would be a rock and a time of partings would be upon us. Indeed, with a family to be educated it seemed very likely that for years and years

155

the children and I would be kept in towns, while Jimmy would be on rocks. I could not bear to think of such a future.

Jimmy studied at home one winter, and in the spring, sat the entrance examinations for Aberdeen University. This successfully over, we bought a house in a neighbouring village, and he resigned from the lighthouse service.

As we drove out and away from the sturdy, encircling walls of our last northern light, it was like leaving the security of a safe and familiar harbour and bracing oneself for the unknown buffetings of the open sea.